OTHER WORKS BY
BRO. FREDRICK EZEJI-OKOYE

CAN I TAKE A LITTLE WINE?

WHO PRAYS FOR THE PASTOR?

NOT WITHOUT THE HEAD

UNDERSTANDING YOUR HUSBAND

FREDRICK EZEJI-OKOYE

Carpenter's Son Publishing

Published by Carpenter's Son Publishing, Franklin, TN

Published in association with Larry Carpenter of Christian Book Services, LLC

All Scripture quotations, unless otherwise indicated, are taken from The Holy Bible, New International Version ®, NIV ®. Copyright © 1973, 1978, 1984, 2011 by Biblica, Inc. ® Used by permission of Zondervan. All rights reserved worldwide. www.Zondervan.com. The "NIV" and "New International Version" are trademarks registered in the United States Patent and Trademark Office by Biblica, Inc.

®Scripture quotations marked KJV are taken from the King James Version. Public domain.

Scripture quotations marked (ESV) are from The Holy Bible, English Standard Version ® (ESV ®), copyright © 2001 by Crossway, a publishing ministry of Good News Publishers. Used by permission. All rights reserved.

Scripture taken from the New King James Version ®. Copyright © 1982 by Thomas Nelson. Used by permission. All rights reserved. (NKJV®)

Cover Design, Editing, and Interior Design by Adept Content Solutions

Printed in the United States of America

ISBN: 978-1-XXXXXX-XX-X

CONTENTS

FOREWORD

Behind every success story, including a marriage story, there are thorny situations that were overcome. There is no testimony without a test! Marriage is meant to be filled with comfort, ease, prosperity, togetherness, happiness, joy, and peace. Unfortunately, most marriages are not experiencing this, as stories of broken marriages are common today. One of the key reasons is the failure to understand the marriage partner. This book focuses on wives understanding their husbands. Proverbs 14:1 says, "Every wise woman buildeth her house: but the foolish plucketh it down with her hands." This means that wives have a big role to play in keeping their marriages and homes carefully knit together. This is only possible when wives understand their husbands.

In this book, Brother Fredrick Ezeji-Okoye provides insights that will help wives build their dream marriage beds. Backed by scriptures and other people's experiences, he demonstrates that as a wife, you should understand that all your husband wants is *first* that you acknowledge and respect his headship role. Make him part of your decisions. Seek his opinions on matters before you undertake them. Make his feelings a priority. Submission is not a reflection of inferiority or lesser worth. Christ constantly submitted Himself to the will of the Father without giving up an iota of His worth. Submission isn't about your husband having power over you. *Second,* be the helper you were created to be. Proverbs 18:22 says, "Who so findeth a wife findeth a good thing, and obtaineth favour of the LORD." You're in that man's life to help him succeed. The principle is that two are better than one—you are not single. Understand that without a woman, the man is not complete. Partner with your husband to succeed in God's vision concerning your home. *Last,* be the beloved of your husband. Lay the foundation of your marriage on the principles of love in 1 Corinthians 13:4–8, and you will see how that love will conquer all the thorns along the way.

A word of counsel to the wives: no matter your status or position in society, the divine order in your home is not to be broken. Christ is equal in status to the Father but willingly submits Himself to his Father's will. In the same way, women are equal in value and worth to men, since both are created in God's image. But based on God's design, men and women assume different roles in the marriage relationship. Wives, this book will help you maintain your position in your home and be that virtuous woman God ordained you to be.

> **NO MATTER YOUR STATUS OR POSITION IN SOCIETY, THE DIVINE ORDER IN YOUR HOME IS NOT TO BE BROKEN.**

I wholeheartedly recommend this book *Understanding Your Husband* as a must-read by every woman. Your marriage will be blissful in Jesus's name. Amen.

Pastor Benjamin Nebechukwu,
Senior Pastor & founder
The Living Word Assembly, Uganda.

INTRODUCTION

Now and then, men lament that their wives are not submissive to them. "She's disrespectful"; "she doesn't love me"; "she nags all the time"; "she never acknowledges anything good that I do"; "I think that I made the greatest error marrying my wife"; "I can't cope with her anymore." I can go on and on with similar statements by men.

These complaints pave the way for too many men to walk away from the covenant they made—the one where they swore to stay with their wives "till death do us part." This has increased the number of absent fathers in homes, which has caused more harm than good. It is, therefore, the pandemic of our generation today.

Recognizing this pandemic of our generation caused me to write a book titled *Not without the Head: An insightful guide for men to embrace God's instructions for success in marriage, family, and community.*

By His grace, all that is written in that book is transparent enough to inspire men to understand their role of headship in their various families.

However, in the process of publication and immediately after the release of that book came the heavy burden of writing another. This one is to encourage women in helping their men fulfill God's ordained headship role in their lives.

Many battles—or rather, misunderstandings—in marriages today are caused by two people fighting for their rights. The man is busy fighting for submission, and the wife is fighting for love.

Only if the woman understands and sticks to her responsibility and not her rights will things turn out differently for good, and the same goes for men.

As I mentioned, this book is aimed at women this time and not the men, so I will not bore you with the men's issues. By God's grace, I will address important areas to consider as encouragement for our ladies, to help win this battle over the absence of fathers in homes.

For the ladies to get involved in this battle, I felt there should be a sincere truth aired. That is why this book is titled *Understanding Your Husband*. Knowledge is so vital in the institution of marriage. But ironically, many find themselves in a marriage without adequate knowledge of marriage itself.

Equality and Authority

Then God said, "Let us make mankind in our image, in our likeness, so that they may rule over the fish in the sea and the birds in the sky, over the livestock and all the wild animals, and over all the creatures that move along the ground." So God created mankind in his own image, in the image of God he created them; male and female he created them. (Gen. 1:26–27)

Men and women are created in God's image, equal, and given the same authority to have dominion, to rule. Despite many misinterpretations of this scripture at the rampart, it is obvious that men and women are equal in the eyes of God. Any teaching to the contrary that is being advanced is exactly the plan of the enemy, who knows it is his duty to steal, kill, and destroy. Ladies, never allow any person to talk you out of knowing

> DESPITE MANY MISINTERPRETATIONS OF THIS SCRIPTURE AT THE RAMPART, IT IS OBVIOUS THAT MEN AND WOMEN ARE EQUAL IN THE EYES OF GOD.

and holding this truth. You're created equally and given authority to rule over creatures. However, read in between the lines—you have the authority to rule the creature and not man. The man has no authority to rule over the wife; neither does the woman have the authority to rule over the man. There's a lot of fighting going on today based on this misinterpretation of who rules over whom.

Understanding the Role Functions between the Man and the Woman

Now no shrub had yet appeared on the earth and no plant had yet sprung up, for the LORD God had not sent rain on the earth and there was no one to work the ground, but streams came up from the earth and watered the whole surface of the ground. Then the LORD God formed a man from the dust of the ground and breathed into his nostrils the breath of life, and the man became a living being.

Now the LORD God had planted a garden in the east, in Eden; and there he put the man he had formed. The LORD God made all kinds of trees grow out of the ground—trees that were pleasing to the eye and good for food. In the middle of the garden were the tree of life and the tree of the knowledge of good and evil.

A river watering the garden flowed from Eden; from there it was separated into four headwaters. The name of the first is the Pishon; it winds through the entire land of Havilah, where there is gold. (The gold of that land is good; aromatic resin and onyx are also there.) The name of the second river is the Gihon; it winds through the entire land of Cush. The name of the third river is the Tigris; it runs along the east side of Ashur. And the fourth river is the Euphrates.

The LORD God took the man and put him in the Garden of Eden to work it and take care of it. And the LORD God commanded the man, "You are free to eat from any tree in the garden; but you must not eat from the tree of the knowledge of good and evil, for when you eat from it you will certainly die."

The LORD God said, "It is not good for the man to be alone. I will make a helper suitable for him." Now the LORD God had formed out of the ground all the wild animals and all the birds in the sky. He brought them to the man to see what he would name them; and whatever the man called each living creature, that was its name. So the man gave names to all the livestock, the birds in the sky and all the wild animals.

But for Adam no suitable helper was found. So the LORD God caused the man to fall into a deep sleep; and while he was sleeping, he took one of the man's ribs and then closed up the place with flesh. Then the LORD God made a woman from the rib he had taken out of the man, and he brought her to the man. The man said, "This is now bone of my bones and flesh of my flesh; she shall be called 'woman,' for she was taken out of man." (Genesis 2:5–23)

I can only explain this with the scriptures. I think this is where the misconception comes in. Equality should never substitute roles. The woman is equal to the man, but both have different roles to function amicably when it comes to marriage.

The headship role is given to the man and not to the woman. The woman came in to be the *helper*. Once a woman understands and embraces the mystery behind this scripture, it will, by the grace of God, bring out the very best in her husband.

God's design was never that a woman was inferior or a secondary person, but instead, she is a co-laborer who is equal but playing different roles to achieve God's ordained marriage.

Understanding Your Husband

From the experiences I have had the privilege to encounter in the Men's Ministry, it became clear to me that every woman is dealing with two different personalities in men. Each of the two personalities seeks the same need from the wife, but each reacts differently. The two personalities of men I'm referring to here are:

1. **The outpouring type of men**: These men are naturally outpouring when it comes to expressing themselves. They are kind but

very loud and very passionate about expressing their views. They easily get angry but are very quick to calm down when their needs are met. When their rights are challenged, they often fight back immediately with harsh words. If there is abuse in the marriage, women who are married to this type of men usually experience verbal abuse

2. **The absorbing type of men:** These men are just the opposite of the outpouring type of men. They don't usually express their feelings. They get irritated when family matters are brought up for deliberations. In other words, they shy away from confrontational discussions. They would rather keep themselves busy with other things just to avoid resolving conflicts. You never know what's on their mind. Though they appear quiet, never mistake that as a weakness. If there is abuse in the marriage, ladies married to this type usually experience physical abuse

As a woman, wherever you find yourself, bear one thing in mind. Men with either type of personality are considered the heads of their homes. Men never lobbied or campaigned for headship—rather, God ordained it to be so. And as the heads of their homes, men with either type of personality have great expectations of their wives. However, a wife can't give what she doesn't understand. That is why it is crucial for ladies to understand headship and how best to deal with it in order to have a peaceful home

Be encouraged as we navigate through this book so you can understand what a man really needs from his wife.

CHAPTER 1

SUBMISSION

Wives, submit yourselves to your own husbands as you do to the Lord.
For the husband is the head of the wife as Christ is the head of the
church, his body, of which he is the Savior. Now as the church submits
to Christ, so also wives should submit to their husbands in everything.
—Ephesians 5:22–24

A wife submitting to her husband is a love language for any type of man existing on Earth, whether the outpouring or the absorbing type of man. All men seek and desire that their wives submit to them.

Ironically, the word *submission* has become the most challenging word ever for most wives. In truth, this is God's principle for the institution of marriage. Submission does not make you inferior, and it does not make you unequal to your husband.

Submission, in this context, simply means that wives acknowledge the headship of their own husbands. God made man the head, and the purpose of his headship is to lead his family. When a woman acknowledges the husband's role as the head, we witness orderliness in the home.

God's words are simple and straightforward but become so difficult when twisted to suit the fleshly desire. My advice is, rather than trying to twist God's instruction, seek the help of the Holy Spirit to enable you to be the *doer* of the word and not just the *hearer*.

Godly wives need the Holy Spirit to enable them to practice the scriptures. God said—and yes, He meant it—that wives should submit to their own husbands as they do unto Him (God). Now I need you, the wife, to pause for a minute and reread the verse above one more time and meditate on it. Contemplate how, on Earth, God will consider the role given to the husband in his home as similar to the role of our Lord Jesus Christ and the Church. This is so huge and deep that when wives understand this scripture, they realize that practicing submission to their husbands is not doing their husbands a favor; rather, it is walking daily in the very will of God concerning their responsibility at home.

Wives, understand that your responsibility is to submit. When that revelation becomes clear to you, ask the Holy Spirit to help you to practice it daily. Without the help of the Holy Spirit, no matter how spiritual you might think you are, you will never authentically yield to this instruction.

I have heard wives say that their husbands do not love them—why submit to a man who doesn't love or care. I also have heard statements like: "These are advanced or modern times" and "We're no longer in the olden days when men subdued women with this scripture on submission." So, wives are now opposing the word of God based on several seemingly good reasons.

But no excuse is good enough to justify disobedience to the Word of God. Once you lean with the Helper (Holy Spirit), you can stay focused on your responsibility rather than seeking to fight for your "right." If wives and husbands focus on fulfilling their responsibilities and ignoring their "rights," peace will reign at home. Your right is for your husband to love you, but your responsibility is for you to submit to his headship.

Again, we're not discussing the responsibility of the husband in this book because we addressed that topic in my previous book, titled *Not without the Head: An insightful guide for men to embrace God's instructions for success in marriage, family, and community.*

Understanding Your Husband is meant to encourage the wives to not kick against God's instruction because of the abuse that's been inflicted by some men. It is very unfortunate to see people twisting God's word to suit them. Twisting God's word does not make it become true. Using the excuse of how men have abused this scripture is also not a reason for you to be disobedient to the will of God.

Understand that your husband is bound to naturally love you when you are showing and living your part—your responsibility of submission to him. The battle begins when the woman is seeking her right to unconditional love before submitting. When addressing men, I mentioned the same to them—a woman will naturally submit when a man loves unconditionally, without first seeking the submission from his wife that he sees as his right.

Recognizing that your husband needs you to acknowledge his headship will save you a lot of trouble at home. Let us fight the good fight of faith and help reduce the rising statistics of the absence of fathers in homes. Misunderstanding the meaning and priority of submission to a husband, which is one of the most important things a man desires from the wife, creates a painful marriage lacking comfort, which has led to many divorces.

> **A WIFE SUBMITTING TO HER HUSBAND IS A LOVE LANGUAGE FOR ANY TYPE OF MAN EXISTING ON EARTH.**

I would like to share true-life stories of three different situations—the reaction of husbands when they felt their wives were not submissive. Unfortunately, many homes have broken up, while many others are enduring but in great pain, based on this issue of submission.

Situation One

The man disconnected from fulfilling his responsibility as husband and father so much that he did not provide for or contribute to the daily needs of his family. It was so bad that even the mortgage, utility bills, and school fees for the kids were all paid by the wife. The wife, of course, couldn't handle it all and began to consider ending the marriage. Meanwhile, the husband had a job that paid well, but he just lived in the house, disconnected. It was so painful hearing this from the wife. When I approached the man, he simply said that his wife didn't talk to him or seek his opinion before doing things. He said she always went ahead, doing what she felt was OK for the family. Why then, would she expect him to do what she's complaining that he is not doing? His response threw me off, but I calmed myself to help understand him more. He went on to explain further what he meant with an example. He said the wife bought their home without his consent, input, or approval simply because she could financially afford it on her own.

Situation Two

This situation is very similar to the first one: The man held a job that paid well, but he was completely disconnected from fulfilling his responsibility of headship. The wife paid the mortgage, utility bills, even school fees for the kids. When I met the man, I asked, "Sir, can you please explain exactly what your wife has done that made you dump paying all household bills on her?" The man's response was a shocker to me. He said the wife made too much money and always had her own agenda. So, he withdrew from his own responsibility to ensure she didn't have enough to spend elsewhere. I requested an example of his wife's reckless spending. He said he wanted to buy their home in a certain location, but his wife preferred a different location. His wife was planning on building the house from scratch in her preferred architectural style and location, so he decided to take the back seat since she wanted to lead.

Situation Three

This situation is different from the other two, but the husband still has similar behavior and disconnects from his wife. The difference here is that the husband was still providing for the family but ignored anything concerning the wife. It was so bad that although they both lived together, they never did anything together. When I had the opportunity to talk with the husband, he gave an example of how his wife didn't yield to his decision on the kind of car he had wanted for her. Instead, she went ahead and bought her choice of car. Both husband and wife shared a home, but in practice they lived their lives individually and separately.

If you read in between the lines in these three situations, you will realize that the husbands were all seeking submission from their wives. Each type of man, whether the outpouring or absorbing, will always appreciate that their wives include them in decision-making. The husbands in these three situations reacted by shutting down or blocking out their wives. I believe and always counsel men that they should love their wives unconditionally, regardless. However, if wives want to focus on fulfilling their responsibilities, they should acknowledge the headship role of husbands. If this acknowledgment of headship happens, there will always be room for compromise in the marriage.

It is very rare for a husband to refuse the heart's desire of his wife if the wife acknowledges the headship of the man. A man is not threatened by the woman's desires but will always be threatened when the woman is not submissive to him with those desires.

Abuse of Submission

I am not an advocate for, and will not be a part of, a man leading the family in the wrong direction and the woman simply submitting. Any leadership heading away from the will of God should not be accepted. God equated the headship of the husband to that of our Lord Jesus Christ. Thus, every husband's headship should look like that of our Lord Jesus Christ, and every woman's submission should be like the church's submission to Christ.

We have also heard some men complain bitterly about their wives' submission to their spiritual leaders or their bosses at their places of work. This kind of situation is found and experienced more in third-world nations. We've seen where wives were more submissive to spiritual leaders than to their husbands. This problem has destroyed many Christian homes. The Bible clearly states that as a wife, you must be submissive to your *own* husband. This discussion was intentionally brought under this subtitle to encourage wives to make submission to their *own* husbands a priority in their marriages. The scripture specified your *own* husband; placing anyone other than your husband first is an abuse.

When a husband feels threatened by your passion for and zealous service to the church, always remember to make the effort to show him that his opinion on your decision matters. When you respect his opinion, he feels that he is your priority. Again, no man will feel threatened or refuse to let his wife to be of zealous service to the church or in the workplace if he knows that his headship is still acknowledged and respected. Women start having problems once their husbands start feeling that they have no control in the home, their headship is not recognized, or other people are now in control of their wives and homes.

Even in counseling, I advise women to seek some sort of approval from their husbands before embarking on any service they feel like doing for the Lord. When this is done, the man will forever remain cooperative and supportive because his headship is being acknowledged.

Submission Is Accountability

"Two are better than one, because they have a good return for their labor" (Eccles. 4:9).

Truly speaking, submission is all about accountability. God's purpose for submission is all about accountability; it has nothing to do with the wife seeing herself as inferior to the man. In homes where God's ordained principles are practiced, couples navigate smoothly, without any issues. After taking a better look at the situations described earlier, you'll agree with me that if the wives of those three men had submitted their desires to their husbands, together they would've taken time to talk over those desires or pray about them to arrive at amicable decisions. The act of submission would've given those

TRULY SPEAKING, SUBMISSION IS ALL ABOUT ACCOUNTABILITY.

wives better results and saved them the pain they were nursing. That's why the scripture says two are better than one. Where there's no submission, we have two people living as if they were single. Their labor will not be fruitful because they're not united; therefore, they overburden themselves.

Now the serpent was more crafty than any of the wild animals the LORD God had made. He said to the woman, "Did God really say, 'You must not eat from any tree in the garden?'" The woman said to the serpent, "We may eat fruit from the trees in the garden, but God did say, 'You must not eat fruit from the tree that is in the middle of the garden, and you must not touch it, or you will die.'" "You will not certainly die," the serpent said to the woman. "For God knows that when you eat from it your eyes will be opened, and you will be like God, knowing good and evil." When the woman saw that the fruit of the tree was good for food and pleasing to the eye, and also desirable for gaining wisdom, she took some and ate it. She also gave some to her husband, who was with her, and he ate it. (Gen. 3:1–6)

We should learn a huge lesson from this scripture about the fall of Adam and Eve. Adam was right there in the middle of Eve's conversation with the devil. Had Eve submitted to Adam by simply asking Adam what he thought about the idea, who knows, it might have made Adam come back to his senses and remember clearly God's instruction to him. Perhaps that fall could have been prevented. Yes, again, Adam was present and could've stopped it, but since he didn't, that tells us that two are better than one when submission is practiced. There's another popular saying that two wrongs can never make a right. So, wives, be encouraged to share your desires or plans with your husband. Submission keeps you accountable, and accountability is good and a very necessary part of what God ordains for marriage. It's about time wives renew their minds from the twisted meaning of submission and practice the will of God.

Submission Is Acknowledging the Headship Role
"For the husband is the head of the wife as Christ is the head of the church, his body, of which he is the Savior (Eph. 5:23)"

The headship role is not leadership. Everyone (women and men) has the spirit of leadership. There are several potential leadership skills among females and males. There is no contention here about whether women are to lead or not. Women are leaders and great leaders indeed. In the present day, we have a lot of women in leadership positions who are doing extremely well, both in the secular sector and for the kingdom of God. However, being a leader or being in a leadership role is totally different from the role of headship in a marriage. The husband's headship role is the divine order of the institution of marriage.

The man is the head, meaning he is the leader in the home, and the woman's role is to help him lead well. If women understand that submission is acknowledging the headship role, it will help women who are in a leadership position or have not yet submitted to the headship of their husbands. Many women who understand this mystery emerge successful both at home and at their various assignments. Why? Because she has a man whose headship role she accepts and respects, thus he is empowering her spiritually, emotionally, and physically.

Those who misunderstand the mystery behind submission are missing out and are not following the divine order. Many ladies even choose to be single rather than marry and submit. Many marriages have ended in divorce because the women do not acknowledge their husbands' headship in the marriage.

Please be encouraged and understand the difference between leadership and headship. You can definitely practice your leadership role, still be married, and be submissive to the headship role of your husband.

> Now Deborah, a prophet, the wife of Lappidoth, was leading Israel at that time. She held court under the Palm of Deborah between Ramah and Bethel in the hill country of Ephraim, and the Israelites went up to her to have their disputes decided. (Judg. 4:4–5)

Deborah was a great leader, as recorded in the book of Judges, but was still successfully married to her husband, Lappidoth. Deborah understood the difference and was able to have a happy married life regardless of her leadership position.

Not all husbands are in a leadership position, but every husband holds the headship position. Throughout the story recorded in the book of Judges, there was no other place Lappidoth was mentioned apart from the verse saying Deborah was married to him. He never held any leadership position, but Deborah was happily married to him.

Today, many women also hold great leadership positions and are happily married—because they understand the difference between leadership and headship.

There's no argument: women and men are created equal and given the same authority. However, there's a divine order that should not be broken. You can't afford to be out of God's will because of people who twist or abuse Scripture.

Submission Is Reciprocal

"Submit to one another out of reverence for Christ (Eph. 5:21)."

Before winding up this chapter, I would like you to understand that submission is reciprocal. When wives understand that submission is reciprocal, they won't struggle with it. Submission is meant not only for the woman but for the man as well. For there to be a happy and successful married life, couples should submit to one another. Wives ought to submit to the headship role of husbands, and husbands need to submit to their helpers—their wives. Just as the man needs to be respected, the woman also needs to be respected. As the woman needs to be loved unconditionally, the man also needs to be loved unconditionally.

The goal here is for each person to be submissive to their responsibility and stop focusing on their rights. The divine order for the institution of marriage should be considered as a marriage guide. Truly, it's not about your husband but about God's divine order. When wives focus on their responsibility, they will never again see themselves being treated as inferior or being lorded over. There will be no cause for conflicts. God gave the wives roles to play and gave the husbands roles to play because women receive love differently, just as men receive love differently. Men receive

> **THE MAN IS THE HEAD, MEANING HE IS THE LEADER IN THE HOME, AND THE WOMAN'S ROLE IS TO HELP HIM LEAD WELL.**

respect differently, just as women receive respect differently. There should be no need to reject the Word of God simply because of abuse or misinterpretation of Scripture.

I encourage you to take a deep breath, read, and meditate again on this popular scripture. Ask the Holy Spirit to help you focus on your responsibility.

> Submit to one another out of reverence for Christ. Wives, submit yourselves to your own husbands as you do to the Lord. For the husband is the head of the wife as Christ is the head of the church, his body, of which he is the Savior. Now as the church submits to Christ, so also wives should submit to their husbands in everything. Husbands, love your wives, just as Christ loved the church and gave himself up for her to make her holy, cleansing her by the washing with water through the word, and to present her to himself as a radiant church, without stain or wrinkle or any other blemish, but holy and blameless. In this same way, husbands ought to love their wives as their own bodies. He who loves his wife loves himself. After all, no one ever hated their own body, but they feed and care for their body, just as Christ does the church— for we are members of his body. "For this reason a man will leave his father and mother and be united to his wife, and the two will become one flesh." This is a profound mystery—but I am talking about Christ and the church. However, each one of you also must love his wife as he loves himself, and the wife must respect her husband. (Eph. 5:21–33)

When you yield to the Holy Spirit for help, He will help. The Holy Spirit is here on Earth to help us fulfill God's will. Never worry or focus on whether your husband is carrying out his responsibility; rather, worry and focus on doing yours. It's amazing how things turn around for good when each person in a couple focuses on their individual responsibilities as husbands or wives. It's like a magnet. When you work towards maintaining your responsibility without giving up, your husband will naturally respond by keeping his own responsibility without giving up.

Please, never think that I am biased in writing this book. I already have, by His grace, challenged the men to focus on their responsibility and not seeking to obtain their rights from their wives. You can read *Not without the Head: An insightful guide for men to embrace God's instructions for success in marriage, family, and community.*

Together we can restore broken homes and reduce the high rate of absentee fathers in homes.

Shalom!

CHAPTER 2
RESPECT

Wives, respect and obey your husbands in the same way.
Then the husbands who do not obey the word of God will want
to know God. They will want to know God because their wives
live good lives, even though they say nothing about God.
They will see that you live holy lives and respect your husbands.
—1 Peter 3:1–2

The scripture above is rampantly used when men lament ordeals in their marriages. When wives don't respect their husbands, the husband's headship is being challenged, and this often leads to malfunctions in the man's role. When a malfunction in a man's headship role kicks in, the battle of fighting for rights takes over.

Wives should apply the principle of respecting their husbands to win their hearts, especially if their husbands don't know God.

A man recently called, lamenting how disrespectful the wife was to him despite the wife's display of spiritual strength. This disrespect from his wife actually pushed the husband away from Christianity, and that shouldn't happen. As much as I disagreed with the man's decision to question Christianity, wives should understand that being spiritual has no positive impact when they disrespect their husbands. If wives respect their husbands, men will function well in their headship role.

This topic is crucial and challenging, but if you really want to live in harmony with your husband, you have to respect his authority. I said it before and will keep repeating it for emphasis throughout the course of this book—men never lobbied for the position of headship, but God ordained that the man be the head.

Again, respecting your husband's authority does not make you unequal or inferior. Respecting him gives your husband the natural ego he deserves as the head of his home. Respect ought to come willingly from the wives and not from the husbands trying to force it to happen. We've seen many instances where the men are seeking respect and forcing it to happen. That is totally wrong and shouldn't be tolerated. There are many abuses of God's principles; however, we can't disregard God's instructions simply because there are some who abuse them.

What Is Disrespectful to Men

I have heard many times during counseling wives lament that their husbands accuse them of being disrespectful. All these women were sincere about it, but listening to them from a man's perspective, I can easily identify how or why the wives might be mistaken as disrespectful from a man's point of view. Below are a few points to discuss. These points may not relate to all, but in general, they will apply to any type of man. Disrespect is disrespect to any type of man, although each man may react differently. Refer back to the introduction of this book on the outpouring type of man, who reacts differently than the absorbing type of man. However, both types of men view disrespect the same way.

Using harsh words: "A gentle answer deflects anger, but harsh words make tempers flare (Prov. 15:1)."

Anger is the most common temperament among men. When you use harsh words in explaining how you are feeling, it makes matters worse for the man. Yes, I understand it hurts, and he probably keeps repeating the same thing over and over again, but please refrain from harsh words when communicating with your husband. Learn to take a deep breath, think over what you would like to say, and make sure you're in a good mood before approaching your husband. I know that there are some silly and annoying things you can't take lightly, but saying it in the way you feel at the time creates anger. And when this continues, it creates unnecessary havoc at home.

I'm currently working with a man who is considering walking away from his marriage because of his wife's constant use of harsh words. The man said to me that he couldn't handle it anymore. Can you imagine how such issues lead to many of the divorces we're seeing and recording these days?

Trying to change him: "Better to live on a corner of the roof than share a house with a quarrelsome wife. (Prov. 21:9)."

The more you try to change your husband, the more frustrated and quarrelsome you become, unknowingly. Men react quickly, and the action is the opposite of your expectation when you continually try to change them into the kind of man you dream about having. Complaining every day about a behavior that you would love to see him change will never make a difference; rather, it worsens the problem. I have seen some men walk away from their homes and marriages because they couldn't stand their wives' quarrelsomeness anymore. Listening to wives talk during counselling, you can clearly see and understand their angle, which usually makes lots of sense. But I will always encourage ladies to resist trying to change their husbands. You can't change him, but you can change yourself. After reading this book, be determined to not try changing your husband, but rather, try changing yourself first, as "two wrongs can never make a right."

Trying to lead: "But I want you to realize that the head of every man is Christ, and the head of the woman is man, and the head of Christ is God (1 Cor. 11:3)."

I did mention the difference between headship and leadership earlier and will repeat it. Your husband will definitely appreciate your lead on anything you desire to lead concerning the family if you acknowledge his headship. It is disrespectful to him if you decide to lead without his consent. I have seen many homes break down due to the leadership skills the woman possesses. In such instances, the wife is usually a great leader with a go-getter ability, while the husband is the opposite, which makes the wife feel it's proper to go ahead and lead the family too. Inasmuch as what she's doing is with good intention, without the husband's consent, there will always be a problem. Again, many women in leadership positions are happily married because they understand this principle.

Comparing: "We do not dare to classify or compare ourselves with some who commend themselves. When they measure themselves by themselves and compare themselves with themselves, they are not wise (2 Cor. 10:12)."

Marriage is all about complementing and not competing or comparing one another. When you compete with or start comparing yourself to your husband, it destroys the man's ego. You may mean well in your heart when you challenge him to step up. But no matter how well you mean it, you end up being disrespectful in his eyes. Please resist pointing out to him what you did better or how many times you've achieved doing something at which he failed.

> "BUT I WANT YOU TO REALIZE THAT THE HEAD OF EVERY MAN IS CHRIST, AND THE HEAD OF THE WOMAN IS MAN, AND THE HEAD OF CHRIST IS GOD (1 COR. 11:3)."

Another huge area of disrespect is comparing your husband to other people or to the husbands of your friends. This not only destroys the man's ego but also affects his mental faculty as well. When you see things that other husbands do, and you would love to have your husband do the same, never let him know your request or wish is fueled by the fact that you saw someone else's husband do the same. Instead, keep encouraging him with how important it is for him to do so and why you need him to do that. Winning his heart to do what you hope, without comparing him to another man will make him feel honored and that is wisdom at your end.

Despise him not: "See that you do not despise one of these little ones. For I tell you that their angels in heaven always see the face of my Father in heaven (Matt. 10:18)."

In one of our counseling sessions, I could see the lady's frustration as she narrated their conflicts. To her, she was acting right and trying to help the husband. But to the man, the wife was being disrespectful to him. This man had lost his job, and according to him, he was trying his best to secure another job, but things were not working out as he had hoped. So, every time the wife came home with her pressures from work, she will start nagging him about how he's not doing enough job hunting. Hearing from both sides, you can see how frustrating such issues can get. To the wife, he was not trying enough, but to the man, his wife was disrespecting him. No man who loses a job can endure things when he feels his wife is looking down on him. In the situation I mentioned here, the man explained that the wife kept saying loudly, to his face, that all he did was eat and nothing else. Such statements or attitudes push men in the opposite direction. Such a response from their wives makes them feel more isolated; it doesn't help them get back on their feet. If you find yourself in this type of situation, please meditate on the scripture, Matthew 10:18, and put your husband's name in, where the Bible says "one of these little ones." You will definitely be affected, and rather than despising him, you will be praying for him.

Interruption: "My dear brothers and sisters, take note of this: Everyone should be quick to listen, slow to speak and slow to become angry (James 1: 19)."

Avoid interrupting your husband when he is still talking or in the middle of his sentence during a conversation. Even if he's not making any sense or getting to a point, learn to listen to him and allow him to finish. I've seen and heard many communications turn into chaos. The outpouring type of man may become verbally abusive if not controlled, while the absorbing type of man may become physically abusive when such conversations become chaotic.

Please don't get me wrong here. My predictions are based on observations from many

> MY DEAR BROTHERS AND SISTERS, TAKE NOTE OF THIS: EVERYONE SHOULD BE QUICK TO LISTEN, SLOW TO SPEAK AND SLOW TO BECOME ANGRY (JAMES 1: 19)."

cases, especially during counseling sessions with couples. I am not saying all cases end up with the abusive behavior or an outcome as described, but the majority do. Many times, we see the men spending more time elsewhere rather than going home on time, just to stay away from the wife. This has led many married men into becoming alcoholics, spending less time at home, and even having mistresses. Remember, two wrongs cannot make a right. Learn to listen to him when he's talking and try not to interrupt. That does not make you weak but makes you wise.

Exposing his weakness: "The wise woman builds her house, but the foolish pulls it down with her hands (Prov. 14:1)."

Men are always uncomfortable and feel disrespected when their wives expose their weaknesses. This is the major reason why counseling backfires rather than restoring peace when not handled wisely. My advice to ladies is to try resolving issues as much as you can with your husband first, and then carry him along if you think your marriage needs counseling. When men are not carried along before they engage in a counseling session, they feel disrespected. Another common mistake made by wives is exposing your husband's weakness to your family members or your friends. That will never help resolve the issues but will worsen them. Please be wise and know that any weakness your husband struggles with should be handled wisely and maturely. Helping him overcome the weakness is the ultimate motive, but how that happens is beyond your control. Encourage him to attend counseling and explain why you feel counseling is needed. The man will feel respected and will be far more likely to accept counseling than if the wife exposed him before letting him know.

Rejecting his vision: "People may be right in their own eyes, but the LORD examines their heart. (Prov. 21:2)."

While having a discussion, a man lamented that he doesn't understand why his wife always rejects the great ideas he proposes for his family. He felt disrespected by his wife's rejection. I asked him if he meant that she had rejected a particular idea of his, or was it like every idea he brought up. He responded that he couldn't remember any of his ideas the wife had ever agreed with. While he was sharing this information with me, he had already made up his mind to not ever share any of his ideas with his wife because he felt he already knew her reaction. This is a common issue that comes up at counseling sessions. Men feel more respected when their wives encourage them, even when they don't agree with their husband's ideas. Encourage him and share your opinion about why you think differently about his ideas. Never reject an idea outright. At most, after you've aired your thoughts to him, take his ideas to the Lord in prayer. If those ideas are not from the Lord, they will not stand.

I strongly believe that rather than having your husband feel you're not supportive and seeing your sincere opinion as being disrespectful, allow him to follow his ideas and keep praying to God. The Lord examines the heart; He alone can convict a man who is heading the wrong way but thinks he's on the right track. You might disagree with me here, but I can tell you that it works perfectly well. When you surrender your husband's ideas to the Lord and believe in your prayers, if it's of the Lord, it will stand, but if not, it will not stand. God also has a way of teaching men. Most times, men learn from their mistakes. God's ways and our ways are different, and the same is true about His thoughts and our thoughts. God can allow the man to experience the consequences of an action if such ideas are not God's will. Such experiences are great teachers for most men. Trust me, that man will learn more from such an experience than you trying to deter him.

Pride and arrogance: "To fear the LORD is to hate evil; I hate pride and arrogance, evil behavior and perverse speech (Prov. 8:13)."

"I bought the house." "This is my house; you've bought nothing in this home. I make more money than you do." "So, what is your problem?" These words were the ranting I witnessed from a wife, and all the husband could say was, "My wife is so disrespectful to me, and I can't handle it anymore." It's very unfortunate that this happens in many homes and has contributed to many cases of divorces. Pride and arrogance have destroyed many homes. Such attitudes shouldn't be allowed—even God Himself hates them. No matter how annoying the man may be or whatever he may do that might make you react negatively, step back and ask the Holy Spirit to help you. Most negative words you utter may not be intentional or may be out of anger, but they are destructive and once spoken, cannot be taken back.

Public opinion: "Women should remain silent in the churches. They are not allowed to speak, but must be in submission, as the law says. If they want to inquire about something, they should ask their own husbands at home; for it is disgraceful for a woman to speak in the church (1Cor. 14:34–35)."

It is very unfortunate that this scripture has frequently been misinterpreted, denying the leadership skills of women or making them feel unequal or like second-class citizens in Christendom. False interpretations of this scripture cannot be accepted and should not be encouraged. Paul was advising women to always stand with their husbands in his opinions, especially in public places.

In Corinth, there were issues with diverse opinions in the church, which even affected couples who viewed things differently in the church. Generally, the advice encourages unity for couples. Being unified can be a wise thing. A man will feel respected if his wife stands with him in public opinion even if she is viewing things differently. It is better to stand with your husband in public. When you get back home, you can then iron it out with him. We saw similar situations in ancient Corinth that are happening today, where some women become overzealous, speaking contrary to their husbands' opinions publicly. Showcasing yourself as more spiritual than your husband in public places destroys the man's ego. If your opinion is different than your husband's, it is better to keep quiet while in a public gathering rather than challenging him right there. Any type of man would feel disrespected if challenged in public. Again, this scripture doesn't dispute women in leadership! Women are great leaders, and we have many women in leadership who are happily married and are respectful to their husbands

CHAPTER 3
HELPER

The Lord God said, "It is not good for the man to be
alone. I will make a helper suitable for him."
—Genesis 2:18

Men need women to accomplish God's mandate for their lives. In the account of creation, when man was formed, God placed him in the garden, gave him vision, and charged him with instructions. He now went further to introduce a woman to help him.

> The Lord God took the man and put him in the Garden of Eden to work it and take care of it. And the Lord God commanded the man, "You are free to eat from any tree in the garden; but you must not eat from the tree of the knowledge of good and evil, for when you eat from it you will certainly die." (Gen. 2:15–17)

"Show me a successful man and I will show you a prudent woman behind the success of that man." This is a slogan, but very true if we may see it from the biblical point of view. Wives, stay encouraged, and understand that your husband needs you to help him succeed. Without a woman, man is not complete.

Ladies, understand that when you get married to a man, you're in that man's life to help him succeed. Another word for help is *assist*. So, the primary goal for a woman who is married to a man is to assist him in carrying out God's vision concerning their family. Assisting does not make you second-class or unequal; rather, assisting is complementing.

Your vision can never be different from your husband's vision. Your vision will be in line with that of your husband. God gave you a specific vision that will impact lives globally. God will definitely give you a man who has the same vision but needs a woman like you to assist him in carrying out such a vision.

Another word that can be likened to being a helper is *partnership*. Being a helper is partnering with your husband to succeed in God's vision

> **GOD WILL DEFINITELY GIVE YOU A MAN WHO HAS THE SAME VISION BUT NEEDS A WOMAN LIKE YOU TO ASSIST HIM IN CARRYING OUT SUCH A VISION.**

concerning your home. When a woman understands this basic principle, there will not be competition nor unnecessary unrest in marriages. Both the woman and the man are in it together for good. They are to do things together, and in togetherness, they shall conquer.

We've seen many marriages break up for lack of understanding of this basic principle. There are many cases of women divorcing their men because they felt their husbands were keeping them from fulfilling God's purpose in their lives. We also have seen instances where men are divorcing for this same reason. God is not an author of confusion; He is not behind the broken homes, and His plans will never contradict His word. Broken homes happen because, one way or the other, the rules, or rather the guidelines, for marriage were broken.

I will attempt to share below some important areas in the home where the husband needs the help of his wife.

Family Orderliness

Raising kids: "Listen, my son, to your father's instruction and do not forsake your mother's teaching (Prov. 1:8)."

Whenever I counsel couples who are heading towards divorce, the first thing I ask them is whether they have considered the consequences that will affect the innocent kids they brought to this world. Every child needs both the father and the mother in their lives, especially when they're young. No matter how caring a woman is towards a child, that child still needs a father figure to complement the mother. Men and women discipline differently, and the kids receive it differently. Both can say the same thing to their kid, but the kid will perceive it differently from each of the parents.

I recently advised a man whose wife left their marriage about the vital reason why he has to do everything possible to reconcile with the wife. During our discussion, he kept resisting taking steps towards reconciliation and justifying his choice with many excuses. I then mentioned to him that he needed to be aware that no amount of love he shows to the child will make up for that of the mom. You can't deny a kid the mom's tender care and nurturing. This statement caused the young man to stop, ponder, and reflect. This is true. Many kids are wounded by their parents' separation, and this psychologically affects them. The man needs the help of the woman to raise godly kids.

Household activities: "As each has received a gift, use it to serve one another, as good stewards of God's varied grace: whoever speaks, as one who speaks oracles of God; whoever serves, as one who serves by the strength that God supplies—in order that in everything God may be glorified through Jesus Christ. To him belong glory and dominion forever and ever. Amen (1 Pet. 4:10–11)."

Your husband needs you to not only utilize your God-given gifts at home, but to maximize your gifts without compromise. There are many gifts God has given to women, just as He gave many to men. There are no outlined household activities to be done exclusively by either the wife or by the husband. Whoever is more gifted in certain areas should take over. There are many homes where the man is better at doing homework assignments with the kids, while the wife is better with other things. Some men are better cooks, while their wives are better at handiwork at home. The husband and wife complement each other in areas of service. The bottom line is if the husband receives the help he needs at home and the wife also receives the same, the home will function in harmony. Negligence of such in the home has repeatedly caused more harm than good. Remember, the kids are watching both of you, so help your husband live a godly lifestyle at home.

> **YOUR HUSBAND NEEDS YOU TO NOT ONLY UTILIZE YOUR GOD-GIVEN GIFTS AT HOME, BUT TO MAXIMIZE YOUR GIFTS WITHOUT COMPROMISE.**

Family projects: "Two are better than one, because they have a good return for their labor. Eccles. 4:9)."

The way a woman views and analyzes things is different from a man. Ideally, every type of man needs the wife to be a part of any family project. If there's a family project—for example, purchasing a home—the man's interest might be limited on the foundation of the building, structure of the building, taxes, and the overall cost of maintenance. But the woman might be interested in the neighborhood, school district, the number of bedrooms, interior coloring/decorations, and the size of the kitchen. All such interests are crucial, so surely the man will need the help of the woman to balance the equation. Apart from the home purchase used as an example here, it is important to bear in mind that a man might not be stable enough to carry out any family project all by himself. When this is the circumstance, procrastination or neglect of such projects can be witnessed. I recognize that men sometimes embark on projects without consulting with their wives. But as I said earlier, should you have skipped pages or are just glancing through the book, I've addressed the responsibilities of men in my book titled *Not without the Head*. The book you're reading now is meant to help the ladies understand their husbands and not to address issues for men. So, yes, there are men who do their own things without carrying the wives along. Most of the time, this action does not yield good results. Wives, permit me to say that you should also never carry out a family project without involving your husband. Remember, "two wrongs can never make a right."

Family budgets: "Whoever loves money never has enough; whoever loves wealth is never satisfied with their income. This too is meaningless. As goods increase, so do those who consume them. And what benefit are they to the owners except to feast their eyes on them (Eccles. 5:10–11)?"

Just as I have addressed the men in a separate book, here I am addressing the ladies on planning and managing family finances. Having a family budget saves a lot of stress. Many today reject budgeting because of the wish for free will about spending. Spending without budgeting accumulates debt and causes unrest in many homes. In most cases, the couple earns good money monthly, yet they never have enough. Men need prudent wives to help cultivate the habit of budgeting what to spend. Please don't get me wrong—I am not saying women are the ones who spend the most. No, all I am trying to say is that it is far easier when women get involved in budgeting than when men lead on that. I encourage ladies to help their men budget and be a guide to all their family spending. Where each member of the couple makes their money and spends it without jointly budgeting or saving, it causes havoc. No matter how much each member of the couples makes, if they fail to budget properly, what they earn will never be enough.

Provision: "Anyone who does not provide for their relatives, and especially for their own household, has denied the faith and is worse than an unbeliever (1 Tim. 5:8)."

This scripture has been misinterpreted and has been directed at the man alone. We've seen multiple examples where the wife refuses to help the man run the family. Provision, as mentioned in the scripture above, does not refer to money alone but encompasses several areas where provision might be needed. Provision has nothing to do with you putting in extra hours at work for pay. Many times, couples work allocated hours, even extra hours, but end up either giving back in taxes or paying for day care. So, it's an opportunity cost. Provision here means that you should offer whatever you're able that will help reduce costs or get your husband out of a tight or difficult financial situation. This is advisable especially here in the United States, where time is expensive. If you have the time, provide the time to help your husband. If you have the money, why not!

The points discussed above are based on family orderliness. There are other areas where men need help from their wives that will be discussed. Please note that these discussions are based on experiences gathered from biblical counseling and can vary for each couple. My intention here is for you to acquire more knowledge and add to what's working for you to maintain a peaceful and happy marriage. When women stick to their responsibilities and men stick to their responsibilities, it will result in a happier home. This also means all will be working together towards reducing the divorce rate. Many kids will enjoy the blessing of their parents being together as a happily married couple, until death do them part. As much as couples think they feel the pain of the wrong choice of a spouse, the kids feel the pain the more. I will not go into the record statistics here but can assure you that many kids never recover from the pain of broken homes.

Below are few other areas that might be considered minor but are equally important for understanding where men need help:

Never assume your husband knows exactly what you want him to do. At times, we've come across scenarios where the woman assumes and then acts based on those assumptions. Men fall victim to this all the time. Help the man by letting him know exactly what the issues are so there won't be any repetition. Women have the ability to multitask, while men are more focused, doing one thing at a time. I heard an example of this from a woman, about a time she had come back from grocery shopping. She got upset because the husband was right there in the living room, doing something else, while she was struggling

> **NEVER ASSUME YOUR HUSBAND KNOWS EXACTLY WHAT YOU WANT HIM TO DO.**

with bringing in the grocery bags. Of course, the man should've known to jump up to help, not just taking over bringing in those grocery bags but also giving her a good hug of thanks. Unfortunately, the man was carried away with what he had been doing when she got home. The wife assumed the man should know better. That man was physically present but was preoccupied with what he was doing at the time. I am not making excuses for the man; however, I am encouraging ladies to help their men by explaining or telling them exactly what their expectations are, so the situation doesn't repeat itself. Any type of man will amend his ways for next time.

This situation leads to my next point, the point where couples are living the usual **"no worries,"** yet there are worries. When you tell a man there are no worries, to him there really are no worries. Many wives do not engage in communicating the problem verbally but choose to use body language instead. Unfortunately, many men don't pay attention to body language, and those who do might choose to turn a blind eye to it. Help the man resolve any issue you might have with something he's done by stating the exact issues clearly. Remember to not use harsh words when trying to voice the problem. Depending on the type of man you're married to, the outpouring type will listen to you at any time and be ready to resolve the issue right away, as long as you're not coming with harsh words. The absorbing type of man may need a convenient time to listen and assimilate the information. All I can say is that you should be wise and patient. In general, both types of men can be helped to act better if you tell them exactly what you want rather than saying "no worries," when there are indeed worries.

In one of our marriage counseling sessions, I heard a woman speak about encouraging her husband to become the better man that she wants to see in him. I found that statement very interesting and felt it was so true and that it might help other ladies to help their men as well. She mentioned being a lover of gifts and an outgoing person. To help make herself happy, she now always gives her husband her wish list, especially for special occasions, and reminds him to remember to buy her a gift. She also organizes family vacations, fills the husband in with every detail, and reminds him of the vacation closer to the time. Amazingly, she said this has really helped her husband become the better man she so desires to live with for the rest of her life. You can see that those were her husband's weaknesses, but she chose to not let the husband act alone but helped him to do it right! The takeaway is to not compare but to learn how to encourage and help your husband to do those things you want him to be doing. When you approach your husband in love, that man will definitely do anything for you.

Encourage and inspire your husband to be better than how you met him. Remember, that is the primary reason why God sent you to that man. Any type of man receives encouragement better than attempts to "teach" him. Maybe you've been trying to teach your husband something that you know will benefit him and you're receiving backlash from your husband; try using encouragement instead for the same thing and you will win the heart of that man. Men hear their wives more when it is said through encouragement rather than teaching.

Instead of asking the husband to attend a men's conference that you know will benefit him, express your appreciation to him for being an amazing husband and tell him how important it is for him to strive to be better so he can be a good role model to his son and other men around him. When you're done, remind him of the men's conference and allow him to comprehend it. He needs your help to help him do the right thing, but your manner of approach matters.

Support his personal projects as much as you can. Be his number one cheerleader. Nothing empowers a man more than having a wife who supports his dreams. Encourage him more, boast about him anywhere, promote/ and advertise his business, let people know his strengths, and do not expose his weaknesses.

Ladies, try as much as possible to reconcile with your husbands in every conflict. Help the man to deal with his weaknesses. You're the best person to work with him, more than any other person. YouTube videos and books that can help your man grow are better for him than taking him to counseling without agreement. Introduce counseling when things become really bad for both of you and hard to handle. But even at that point, apply wisdom by engaging him in an agreed-upon conversation before introducing

NOTHING EMPOWERS A MAN MORE THAN HAVING A WIFE WHO SUPPORTS HIS DREAMS.

counseling. Allow him to partner with you so both of you can see a neutral counselor. It doesn't flow well when you're the one who introduces a counselor to the man. Counseling flows better when it's the man who introduces counseling, rather than the woman.

Myth

I would like to end this chapter by exposing a widely held but false belief that men feel intimidated when their wives step in to help. The myth can go further, stating that most men don't want their wives to have a career. This widespread myth is false. Women who struggle in their homes are doing so because they lack the knowledge. Men need help from their wives, and men should know they can't be complete without their wives. A man wants the best for the wife, including her career, and of course, the man wants the wife to help him financially if at all possible. Never give the enemy room to feed you wrong information about men. I want you to understand that your husband needs your help and cherishes it the most when you are helping him. Any type of man has great confidence when he has a wife of noble character, regardless of her leadership position.

Please strive to be who God made you to be. Get that education, pursue your career—your husband has no issues with those. Issues arise when you misplace your leadership role with his headship role. A good woman is a good woman, and that's exactly the woman to whom any type of man is willing to submit!

A wife of noble character who can find? She is worth far more than rubies. Her husband has full confidence in her and lacks nothing of value. She brings him good, not harm, all the days of her life. She selects wool and flax and works with eager hands. She is like the merchant ships, bringing her food from afar. She gets up while it is still night; she provides food for her family and portions for her female servants. She considers a field and buys it; out of her earnings she plants a vineyard. She sets about her work vigorously; her arms are strong for her tasks.

She sees that her trading is profitable, and her lamp does not go out at night. In her hand she holds the distaff and grasps the spindle with her fingers. She opens her arms to the poor and extends her hands to the needy. When it snows, she has no fear for her household; for all of them are clothed in scarlet. She makes coverings for her bed; she is clothed in fine linen and purple. Her husband is respected at the city gate, where he takes his seat among the elders of the land. She makes linen garments and sells them, and supplies the merchants with sashes. She is clothed with strength and dignity; she can laugh at the days to come. She speaks with wisdom, and faithful instruction is on her tongue. She watches over the affairs of her household and does not eat the bread of idleness. Her children arise and call her blessed; her husband also, and he praises her: "Many women do noble things, but you surpass them all." Charm is deceptive, and beauty is fleeting; but a woman who fears the LORD is to be praised. Honor her for all that her hands have done, and let her works bring her praise at the city gate. (Prov. 31:10–31)

CHAPTER 4
LONELINESS

The LORD God said, "It is not good for the man to be alone."
—Genesis 2:18a

A young man called me one evening, frustrated and lamenting about his marriage ordeal. All I heard, repeatedly, was that he felt like he was not married. The bottom line of the whole conversation was that the man was married but lonely. Loneliness is one of the catalysts that ignites infidelity, pornography, depression, anxiety, drug addiction, alcoholism, etc. And in all these, a man still never fills in the hole of loneliness.

Nothing can substitute for such a vacuum in a man's life. Many men who found themselves in such behaviors as listed above have even confessed that those ways of escape made their lives even worse than before.

Other men, who are strong in their Christian faith but experience similar loneliness in their marriages, have found ways of escape in religious activities, such as attending different church programs, having fellowship with other brethren, attending seminars, etc. They often seem addicted to work. Some even enroll in one course after another, just to keep themselves busy in order to fill the vacuum created by loneliness in their marriages. These faithful husbands still cry over such loneliness in their marriages.

31

Now the LORD God had formed out of the ground all the wild animals and all the birds in the sky. He brought them to the man to see what he would name them; and whatever the man called each living creature, that was its name. So, the man gave names to all the livestock, the birds in the sky and all the wild animals. But for Adam no suitable helper was found. So the LORD God caused the man to fall into a deep sleep; and while he was sleeping, he took one of the man's rib[1] and then closed up the place with flesh. Then the LORD God made a woman from the rib he had taken out of the man, and he brought her to the man. The man said, "This is now bone of my bones and flesh of my flesh; she shall be called 'woman,' for she was taken out of man." (Gen. 2:19–23)

Genesis 2:18 says, "The LORD God said, 'It is not good for the man to be alone. I will make a helper suitable for him.'" God, before providing the helper, which we discussed in the previous chapter, first provided other things to see if those would fill the vacuum of loneliness. Although Adam was busy with those other things, there was no intimacy. The vacuum of loneliness was still there until the Lord provided the helper—woman. That brought a sigh of relief to Adam. Woman, the helper, completed the man, and he never hid his expressions of how he felt. He became complete.

No man can be a complete man without a woman. It is not good for a man to be alone, and he needs a helper. Wives fill in this vacuum. Nothing else can fill it but the man's wife. No other woman can fill it—only the right woman for the man. It must be the bones and flesh of the man's flesh, and that is called wife!

Wives, be encouraged; understand that most cases when a man malfunctions are often traces of loneliness. When you fill this vacuum, your husband will get back to himself. Never allow your husband to feel lonely. Lean on the Holy Spirit to help you.

> **WIVES, BE ENCOURAGED; UNDERSTAND THAT MOST CASES WHEN A MAN MALFUNCTIONS ARE OFTEN TRACES OF LONELINESS.**

I know that there are many ugly situations out there, but I beg you—surrender those issues to the Lord. Focus on your responsibility to fill in the vacuum of your husband's life so he can think right and act right. He is not complete without you.

Family priority: "That is why a man leaves his father and mother and is united to his wife, and they become one flesh (Gen. 2:24)."

This Bible verse is a clear indication of family priority. A man's primary focus should be his family first, before the extended family. When a woman stays more attached to her parents or siblings than to her husband, it affects the man. Couples should understand that their own immediate family should be their priority. We have seen cases where the wife takes advice from the parents, contrary to the husband's wishes. Such actions weaken the authority of the man. When you're not united with your husband in all decision-making for your immediate family, the man feels detached, and loneliness might kick in. Nobody will advise you to not visit your parents or siblings, but when those visits take too much time away from your husband, there's a problem. Nobody will advise you to not allow your parents to visit, but if the visit becomes permanent, without your husband's consent, it is a problem. We've seen cases where homes are broken simply because a man feels the wife is still attached to her parents and siblings.

Friendship: "One who has unreliable friends soon comes to ruin, but there is a friend who sticks closer than a brother (Prov. 18:24)."

When the wife makes her husband her best friend, it can resolve loneliness in a man. Some ladies are so occupied with their girlfriends that they spend too much time spent with them and rob their husbands of their companionship. Ladies, your girlfriends should not take priority over your husband's time. A man needs platonic love from the wife. He needs a woman who cares about him. During counseling, we have witnessed a wife complaining that the husband was never home, but the man responded that it was because she was always on the phone with her friends. The man felt lonely but never expressed that to the wife. The act of friendship between couples develops strong bonding.

Intimacy: "Do not deprive each other of sexual relations, unless you both agree to refrain from sexual intimacy for a limited time so you can give yourselves more completely to prayer. Afterward, you should come together again so that Satan won't be able to tempt you because of your lack of self-control (1 Cor. 7:5)."

In counseling, issues of sexual denial are fast increasing and causing damage in more than several homes. I am strongly against sexual abuse of wives by their husbands, and talked about this in my book, *Not without the Head*. However, I would like to encourage the ladies to not deliberately deny their husbands sex. As the Bible verse explained clearly, let any refraining from sex be based on mutual agreement. When it is not mutual, many men have taken the route of infidelity, some to pornography. However, none of these filled the gap of missing intimacy with their wives. Wives, please be encouraged to do everything within your reach to keep the intimate relationship with your husband active.

Time: "Making the best use of the time, because the days are evil (Eph. 5:16)."

These days, it is very important to make the best use of every bit of time given to us. As I pointed out earlier, a man has no problem with a wife's career or leadership position. But any type of man would have concerns if your work or your career takes most of your time away from your family. In most cases, this issue is more prevalent with men, but it is increasing among women. We've heard of a case where a wife was juggling two jobs. The husband went out in the morning to work and upon his return, his wife was still at work. Even spending time together on weekends was rare for both of them. This is detrimental not only to the relationship between the man and the woman but also to the kids. Making the best use of time is crucial and so important. When a man starts feeling uncomfortable about your absence from home, please try as much as possible to adjust. We have also witnessed such instances

MAKING THE BEST USE OF TIME IS CRUCIAL AND SO IMPORTANT.

when women are overzealous with their church duties. Never let your overzealousness for church work take you away from fulfilling your family responsibilities. God is not an author of confusion. Our God is a God of order. Many have lost their marriages, thinking they're serving the Lord. If you are a married woman, time invested in your family should be considered your primary ministry. Paul addressed this issue in 1 Corinthians 7:34–35:

> [A]nd his interests are divided. An unmarried woman or virgin is concerned about the Lord's affairs: Her aim is to be devoted to the Lord in both body and spirit. But a married woman is concerned about the affairs of this world—how she can please her husband. I am saying this for your own good, not to restrict you, but that you may live in a right way in undivided devotion to the Lord.

Togetherness: "Do two walk together unless they have agreed to do so (Amos 3:3)?"

Men feel lonelier in homes where couples live together but do things differently. Nothing brings completion to a man like doing things in togetherness and agreement with the wife. There's a myth out there that men like doing things alone. We have seen rare occasions of this happening, but in most cases, a deep look at such occurrences reveals situations where the orderliness of the marriage was broken. For example, when women consistently disrespect their husbands or speak harsh words to them, such men withdraw. You would notice this a lot among the absorbing type of men. Withdrawal and doing things on their own become the only options. However, it is not the will of God concerning man. Couples are advised to cultivate the habit of doing things together.

Lack of interest: "Do nothing out of selfish ambition or vain conceit. Rather, in humility value others above yourselves, not looking to your own interests but each of you to the interests of the others (Phil. 2:3–4)."

Value your husband's areas of interest. Women who develop an interest in and value the things their men enjoy bond easily. Husbands appreciate their wives more when they are interested in the kind of leisure time the husbands like. Couples who embrace leisure time together are closer in their relationship than those who do not. In adverse cases, men feel the pain of loneliness more.

This also applies to interest in the place of worship. We have seen more incidents these days where the wife goes to a different church than the one the husband attends. Many wives complain about that their spirits feel unfulfilled at the husband's place of worship. However, we will always counsel a woman to attend the same church together, but prayerfully convince the husband where and why they should move. Better still, there's nothing wrong with attending your family church together as a family and then attending your own church of interest afterward, as long as your husband is aware.

> **WOMEN WHO DEVELOP AN INTEREST IN AND VALUE THE THINGS THEIR MEN ENJOY BOND EASILY.**

Lack of encouragement: "Therefore encourage one another and build each other up, just as in fact you are doing (1 Thess. 5:11)."

Nothing empowers a man more than being encouraged by his wife. A man's greatest cheerleader is an encouraging wife. Men seek refuge at home. If he had a bad day or got messed up in any kind of endeavor, but has a woman who will keep his faith strong by encouraging him, that man does exploits. The reverse is the case when a man doesn't get encouragement from his wife. You will find an encouraging wife beside the successful man. There was a story of a prominent business tycoon who, before attaining his height of success, wanted to quit because he had failed in an initial business transaction. To make matters worse, the bank refused

> **A MAN'S GREATEST CHEERLEADER IS AN ENCOURAGING WIFE.**

to give him another loan and demanded repayment of the earlier loan. This man gave up, but not his wife. The wife kept encouraging him and suggested they go to a different bank with the business proposal. Long story short, this other bank granted him the loan, which was reinvested in the same business that had failed earlier, and it is thriving today. This is the power of what encouraging wives can do for men. Understand that words of encouragement trigger positive effects in a man's personality, and they are more powerful when they come from the wife! "Not giving up meeting together, as some are in the habit of doing, but encouraging one another—and all the more as you see the Day approaching" (Heb. 10:25).

Rigidity: "Accept one another, then, just as Christ accepted you, in order to bring praise to God (Rom. 15:7)."

You can't change your husband's personality. The more you try, the more you keep your husband isolated from functioning as the head of the family. Accepting him the way he is makes life easier for both him and you. In a worst-case scenario, take it to the Lord in prayers. Never try to win all battles when there's an issue or conflict. Be flexible, and allow your man to have his way sometimes, even when you feel otherwise. Homes where the woman refuses to be flexible by accepting the husband for who he is create loneliness in such a man's life. Avoid unnecessary harboring of malice with your husband. This attitude keeps the man uncomfortable and makes him feel isolated. Again, circumstances such as these open the door for ungodly acts that trap men. I'm not saying this should be an excuse for men, but I am saying that you, the wife, have a part to play. Try

AVOID UNNECESSARY HARBORING OF MALICE WITH YOUR HUSBAND.

winning the heart of your husband by resolving any conflict immediately rather than keeping malice. Don't let the sun go down on your anger.

CHAPTER 5

TRANSPARENCY

For God will bring every deed into judgment, including
every hidden thing, whether it is good or evil.
—Ecclesiastes 12:14

Let nothing be done in secrecy in your matrimonial home. Secrecy has destroyed many happily married couples. There should be nothing hidden from your husband—no secret money, communications with your friends or family members, trips, health issues, purchases, debt, projects, etc.

Let us look at a few examples of such secrecy kept among couples, which have caused issues in more than a few homes. For the purpose of this book, these examples reflect on the wives, but that does not mean that the men are not equally guilty.

Example 1:

A wife was executing a huge building project without the husband's knowledge. The project was nearing completion when the husband accidentally came across a money transfer receipt for a transaction between the wife and her brother. It was a big shock to this man, and that home was never the same after that. This also applies to wives who hide their account balances from their husbands. Men, as I have emphasized earlier on, have no problem with how much you make, but when you begin to hide how much you make or have, it brings havoc into the home. Men are very sensitive when they realize their wives are hiding their account balance or monetary worth. I recognize there are a few men out there who choose not to do anything but sit and swipe their wives hard-earned money. Such behavior is not ideal and should not be exhibited by responsible men.

Example 2:

A husband and the wife agreed on working out their indebtedness so they could be free from financial bondage. It was a mutual agreement, but at the end of the day, the wife still fell back into extravagant spending, which meant she was using her credit card without the husband's knowledge. The husband found out about it when he received mail from the credit card company. He opened the mail and saw the credit balance. His wife showed no remorse, and that wrecked their home. Couples should be as transparent as possible when it comes to financial matters.

Example 3:

A husband and the wife planned for a family vacation. Prior to their vacation trip, she went to the clinic for her regular check-up. The doctor requested that she get an ultrasound of her thyroid. She went in to have the ultrasound but canceled when she realized the cost. Her decision was based on the fact that the medical bill would affect their vacation trip, and she concealed this information from the husband so the trip could go ahead. Such deceit should not be seen among married couples.

Example 4:

A woman had a friend that she said was her prayer partner. She kept the relationship secret; she never introduced this friend to the husband. However, the husband found out from the neighbors that a lady would usually come around when he was at work and the wife would sneak her out from the back door whenever he came back from work. This husband confronted his wife with this information. That was when she mentioned the woman was her prayer partner. Now, the million-dollar question for this young man was, what kind of prayers were you both praying that you left me in the dark? What caused the difficulty in introducing this prayer partner to him? There are no issues with having prayer partners, but it is very important that your husband is aware of these partners. When your friends or prayer partners are hidden from your husband, that friendship is not healthy for you or your family.

How to Practice Being Transparent

Openness: "Adam and his wife were both naked, and they felt no shame (Gen. 2:25)."

In reading the scripture above, I hope it gives you an understanding that God will judge every deed. It is, therefore, very important to begin renewal of your mind and practice openness with your husband. Openness can be likened to the intimacy you share with your husband. With intimacy, nothing is covered (naked), and neither of you can be ashamed. Practice not keeping things away from your husband. Carry him along with your thoughts, plans, or ideas. Seek his consent on things you intend to do and ensure that nothing is hidden. We are now in the era where different devices—ranging from smartphones to iPads, e-notebooks, etc.—are used and password protected. Your access word should be transparent to your

PRACTICE NOT KEEPING THINGS AWAY FROM YOUR HUSBAND.

husband. The issue of hiding passwords from a spouse is more common among men, but we are beginning to see this crop up among women too. This isn't right and is not good practice for couples. A lot of negative imagination and false accusations come up among couples who are not transparent with their passwords.

Make your passcodes available so your husband feels free to access any of your password-protected devices. In most cases, husbands don't bother with accessing their wives' gadgets except when insecurity exists. Practice openness even when taking calls from a friend or family. At no time should you leave the presence of your husband to answer a call. This should happen only if the conversation might disturb your husband. Little things like this have caused a lot of issues in homes.

Communication: "Let your speech always be gracious, seasoned with salt, so that you may know how you ought to answer each person (Col. 4:6)."

Some wives refrain from having certain types of conversations with their husbands based on not-so-good past experiences. Do not choose to go with this option. Instead, approach your husband at the right time, with the right words, and this draws his attention to you. The more couples communicate with each other, the more transparent they become. This will make for comfortable, even relaxed criticism from each other. For example, it allows you to freely tell your husband how you feel about his unkempt clothing or that he should change his pants if they are dirty. Your husband will appreciate you more than if you are in the habit of concealing things from him. He should hear it from you that his pants need changing rather than from someone else. As mentioned earlier, men may not take corrections well at first, but if your speech is seasoned, you will get a better reaction. Build a relationship in which both of you feel free around each other at all times. If you perceive body odor, encourage him to use deodorants or cologne, or even buy it for him. If his breath is not fresh, encourage him to deep clean with the dentist and to use mouthwash. You shouldn't shy away from honest and useful criticism of your husband on anything at all. That is what I call transparency. Couples should be transparent with each other.

> YOU SHOULDN'T SHY AWAY FROM HONEST AND USEFUL CRITICISM OF YOUR HUSBAND ON ANYTHING AT ALL.

Truth: "Whoever speaks the truth gives honest evidence, but a false witness utters deceit (Prov. 12:17)."

Always maintain the truth, regardless of how your husband might feel or react. Men may respond negatively to hearing the truth but will truly appreciate you afterward for saying the truth. The truth sets us free from bondage. Don't take to lying. It may cover up problems temporarily, but in the long run, it always backfires. You will not have any difficulty recollecting what you said at any given time if you said the truth. The truth will not only set you free but will also strengthen your relationship. It is an honor and a privilege for any type of man to have a wife of integrity. Many times during counseling, we've seen instances when a wife admits to not being truthful to the husband because he would not agree with her. Such a decision actually does more harm than good. The husbands usually feel bad when they hear the truth that is being kept from them. Regardless of how your husband will react, whether his response will be yes or no, please ladies, be encouraged to always tell your men the truth. Saying the truth also sets a good example to the kids. Those kids are watching the relationship between their parents. Saying the truth also applies to things regarding the kids. Do not, out of pampering your kids, hide things away from your husband simply because you feel your husband might be too harsh on the kids. It takes two to raise the kids. When there's a need for correction, please don't handle it all by yourself—involve your husband so both of you can determine the level of discipline or correction needed at that time.

Confession: "Therefore confess your sins to each other and pray for each other so that you may be healed. The prayer of a righteous person is powerful and effective (James 5:16)."

As long as we are human beings, we will fall short of doing what is right. Confessing to each other when we fall keeps us on the right track and helps to build more trust in relationships among us. Some people think that confession might make things worse, but I believe that when you confess to each other, you are building more trust in your relationship. A wife who sincerely confesses to the husband anything she might have done will easily win the heart of the husband. She will also have her conscience cleared. When you confess things you did, you will never want to repeat them. If you've been keeping things away from your husband—maybe you've been financially helping your parents, siblings, or friends without your husband's knowledge—confessing to him will not worsen the situation; rather it will help make the trust you both share stronger. As I said, nothing can be hidden permanently. It's just a matter of time until it is exposed. Marriages have been broken because of hidden agendas that were eventually exposed. There's no hidden wrong that when confessed cannot be forgiven. We've seen truly bad cases, such as infidelity, forgiven because of confession. Confession cannot be compromised on any level or situation. It frees you and allows your conscience to be at peace with your husband and your Creator.

> **MARRIAGES HAVE BEEN BROKEN BECAUSE OF HIDDEN AGENDAS THAT WERE EVENTUALLY EXPOSED.**

Oneness: "The man said, 'This is now bone of my bones and flesh of my flesh; she shall be called 'woman,' for she was taken out of man.' That is why a man leaves his father and mother and is united to his wife, and they become one flesh (Gen. 2:23–24)."

I have no choice but to repeat this scripture again. Wives, be encouraged to always be in unison with your husbands on all plans. Practicing oneness leaves no room for hidden things, and realizing that you both are now one eliminates secrets. Intentionally organize, plan, and do things together. Joint running of family bank accounts easily eliminates secret purchases, expenses, or savings. Couples are encouraged to operate family projects jointly from a joint account and individual projects from individual accounts. At the same time, make your individual bank accounts available to each other. No huge transactions, either family or individual, should be hidden. Once a man is married to you, that man is united with you. There should not be any kind of "me, myself, and I" mentality, for two have become one! Get involved in ministry, business, or anything else—together.

> **ONCE A MAN IS MARRIED TO YOU, THAT MAN IS UNITED WITH YOU.**

Develop the managerial skills in managing family affairs, ministry, or business together with your husband. Let nothing be planned or done separately. It is very hard for couples who practice oneness to have hidden agendas. Such couples have a transparent lifestyle, and they enjoy their marriage in full.

Avoiding assumption: "Casting down imaginations, and every high thing that exalteth itself against the knowledge of God, and bringing into captivity every thought to the obedience of Christ (2 Cor. 10:5)."

Assuming things about your husband is a terrible thing to do. Never assume and then keep it to yourself without letting your husband know. The battle, the negative thought playing with your mind, ought to be cast down. Keeping assumptions to yourself without the knowledge of your husband causes more harm than good. If you suspect that your husband is doing something improper, rather than holding back those assumptions, open up and let him know what's on your mind.

I've seen cases where the man was accused of infidelity without proof. The wife assumed he was having an affair and didn't question him about it. Such behaviors usually affect the marital relationship. Cast down imaginations and avoid accusations without proof. Be encouraged to not keep such assumptions to yourself. Seek your husband's attention and pour out your heart to him. It's better to say it out loud and then hear him out. Do not embark on any search for proof just to justify your assumption when you have not discussed it yet with your husband. Two wrongs can never make a right. It is unfair to your husband if you keep your assumption to yourself and at the same time investigate him without his knowledge. Such actions create distrust in marital relationships. We all are human and are bound to wrestle with our imagination daily. We overcome this by exposing our thoughts in a healthy discussion with our spouse and praying against such thoughts. This is why the Bible talks of casting down imaginations. It's a battle, and you ought to

> IF YOU SUSPECT THAT YOUR HUSBAND IS DOING SOMETHING IMPROPER, RATHER THAN HOLDING BACK THOSE ASSUMPTIONS, OPEN UP AND LET HIM KNOW WHAT'S ON YOUR MIND.

win this war. Resist keeping assumptions to yourself and learn to pour them out. It is not a sin to assume things, but don't bottle it up within you. Share it with your husband and in most cases, pray together.

Avoiding gossipers: "A gossip betrays a confidence; so avoid anyone who talks too much (Prov. 20:19)."

Avoid any friend or group of friends that talk about only their husband's weaknesses. Such a relationship is not healthy and doesn't help you with transparency. Any discussion you have with your friend that can't be shared with your husband shouldn't happen. Anything concerning you and your husband is meant for both of you. No other person should get involved except in circumstances like counseling. Even in counseling, the man should be aware. I keep saying it and will continue repeating it—you should never embark on any kind of counseling without the knowledge of your husband. Just as I stated earlier, that assumption should be avoided; the same goes for gossip. Sometimes, negative information comes your way to haunt you, especially when you are already nursing such thoughts. Don't ever keep it to yourself when you hear negative information; make sure you share it with your husband, at least to hear from him. Gossip has caused a lot of strife and confusion among couples. The Bible says in Proverbs 26:20, "Without wood a fire goes out; without a gossip a quarrel dies down." Gossip is terrible and should be avoided by all means.

CHAPTER 6

LOVE

Whoever claims to love God yet hates a brother or sister is a liar.
For whoever does not love their brother and sister, whom they have seen,
cannot love God, whom they have not seen. And he has given us this
command: Anyone who loves God must also love their brother and sister.
—1 John 4:20–21

Love Is the Nature of God

The Bible makes us understand that God is love. If He is love, we ought
to be love as well. Why? Because He created us male and female in
His own image, therefore we all—both men and women—desire and
expect to be loved. The biblical marriage guide stipulated in Ephesians
is based on concentrating on areas of responsibility and not neglecting
each other. A woman, instructed to respect her husband, should expect
to be respected as well. A man who is instructed to love unconditionally also expects to be loved unconditionally. That's why Paul's opening
statement of the marriage guidelines as recorded in Ephesians 5 starts
with submitting to one another, "Submit to one another out of reverence for Christ (Eph. 5:21)." This verse is crucial to marriage, and it is
important to understand it before moving on to subsequent verses in the
chapter. Often, we hear things like "men are to love but not to respect
their wives" or "ladies are to respect their husbands and not to love

47

them." It is very unfortunate that believers have interpreted this scripture out of context. Men do need love, just as ladies need love. It is very important that as we focus on our responsibilities as in the Ephesians marriage guide. We should not forget that we receive what we give.

Love Is Knowing God, and Love Has No Fear

Knowing God is understanding that He is love. If we've been created in His own image, we ought to be love. He empowers us to love, and our helper, the Holy Spirit, is always present to help you love your husband unconditionally if you surrender to the Holy Spirit. Love should be practiced first at home, before it can be extended to neighbors

WE SHOULD NOT FORGET THAT WE RECEIVE WHAT WE GIVE.

and communities. We ought to love our spouses because we are the same in nature as God. Look around you and see the unconditional love you enjoy from God. We are expected s to give the same one another. We hear things like "I used to love him but not anymore, because I am afraid he will abuse it." The devil puts all sorts of negative images in our heads or uses those ugly pasts to challenge our true nature of love, but I dare you to stick to God's love. God's love fears nothing. Know God and understand that He is love.

Dear friends, let us love one another, for love comes from God. Everyone who loves has been born of God and knows God. Whoever does not love does not know God, because God is love. This is how God showed his love among us: He sent his one and only Son into the world that we might live through him. This is love: not that we loved God, but that he loved us and sent his Son as an atoning sacrifice for our sins. Dear friends, since God so loved us, we also ought to love one another. No one has ever seen God; but if we love one another, God lives in us and his love is made complete in us. This is how we know that we live in him and he in us: He has

GOD LIVES IN US AND HIS LOVE IS MADE COMPLETE IN US.

given us of his Spirit. And we have seen and testify that the Father has sent his Son to be the Savior of the world. If anyone acknowledges that Jesus is the Son of God, God lives in them and they in God. And so we know and rely on the love God has for us. God is love. Whoever lives in love lives in God, and God in them. This is how love is made complete among us so that we will have confidence on the Day of Judgment: In this world we are like Jesus. There is no fear in love. But perfect love drives out fear, because fear has to do with punishment. The one who fears is not made perfect in love. We love because he first loved us. (1 John 4:7–19)

Love Means Loving Yourself

Most times, when we see people struggle with love, it is because they have issues with loving themselves. There's no way you can give what you don't have. We've seen cases where wives just don't love their husbands, not because the husband is the worst man ever, but simply because the wife does not love herself. It is important to understand that for you to flow in the river of love in a marriage, you must stay connected to the source of love. Remember, God first loved you; therefore, love God with everything within you. When you're connected to God and loving Him for who He is and not for what you're receiving, you'll see yourself swimming in love. Love God with all your heart, soul, and strength, and you will never lack love to give. That is why Jesus responded that the greatest among the commandments given is to love God and love our neighbors as we love ourselves.

> Jesus replied: "'Love the Lord your God with all your heart and with all your soul and with all your mind.' This is the first and greatest commandment. And the second is like it: 'Love your neighbor as yourself.' All the Law and the Prophets hang on these two commandments." (Matt. 22:37–40)

Love Is God's Command

Love is not based on human feelings but on God's command. John 14:15 states, "If you love me, keep my commands." God expects us to love if we claim that we love Him (God). Human feelings change from time to time, but God's command never changes, regardless of the circumstance. If you allow yourself to love your husband based on how you feel, you will definitely end up not loving him. Guess what? When you love your husband based on how you feel, it means you're walking in disobedience to the will of God. I totally agree that your husband can be annoying or possibly do very upsetting things; the command is to love him. You might be fuming right now as you're reading this chapter, saying to yourself that this author does not understand what you're going through in your marriage. As much as I do sympathize and agree with how you might be feeling, the truth is that we're not to allow how we feel to determine if we're to be obedient to the will of God or not.

> A new command I give you: Love one another. As I have loved you, so you must love one another. By this everyone will know that you are my disciples, if you love one another. (John 13:34–35)

Love Must Be Sincere

You might not like those ugly character traits of your husband but be sincere to yourself and love him for who he is. No matter how bad someone is, there's always something good about the person. There's nothing wrong with disliking his bad behaviors, but do not let that deter your love towards him. Honor your husband for who he is. We read in Romans 12:9–10, "Love must be sincere. Hate what is evil; cling to what is good. Be devoted to one another in love. Honor one another above yourselves." When you give your husband love, he will receive it and won't need you to physically spell it out to him. However, you may find yourself struggling and lamenting, "I love my husband but he's not getting it; something must be wrong somewhere." Many times, what you hear yourself say might not be exactly what you do. Your husband is in the best position to acknowledge that you love him. What you give him will be what he's receiving.

Love Is Appreciation

Love is being appreciative of who your husband is or thankful for his unique personality. Earlier, I mentioned being sincere, and yes, be sincere about your love and appreciate him for his areas of strength. If your husband is not good about taking you out on a date, appreciate him if he is helping with domestic chores at home. Don't focus on those areas where he is not good, but focus on his strengths and appreciate him.

Be thankful to God for who your husband is. When you're focused on appreciating him for his strengths, love will manifest as it flows. Admire and appreciate those things he's good at doing. Give him warm hugs and kisses, and brag about your king. Speak energetic words that should stir up his ego and make him want to grab you to bed. Let him know how you and the kids feel about him. That makes a man feel loved.

> **WHEN YOU'RE FOCUSED ON APPRECIATING HIM FOR HIS STRENGTHS, LOVE WILL MANIFEST AS IT FLOWS.**

Kiss me and kiss me again, for your love is sweeter than wine. How pleasing is your fragrance; your name is like the spreading fragrance of scented oils. No wonder all the young women love you! Take me with you; come, let's run! The king has brought me into his bedroom. How happy we are for you, O king. We praise your love even more than wine. How right they are to adore you. (Song of Sol. 1:2–4)

Love Is Kind

Love is always speaking kind words to your husband. There is power behind every kind word you speak. I have discussed how men kick against being corrected by their wives. But I can say without mincing words that wives who understood the power of kind words have corrected their husbands on many occasions, without their husbands knowing that they just received correction because they received correction in kind words. I can't help but keep saying it—resist using harsh words, no matter how angry you are; instead, refrain from talking at that moment. Sleep on it and choose the right words when you've cooled

> **THERE IS POWER BEHIND EVERY KIND WORD YOU SPEAK.**

down. Speak kind words to your husband and encourage him more. Kindness is such a powerful love language that a man receives from his wife that it cannot be compromised at all.

> Do not let any unwholesome talk come out of your mouths, but only what is helpful for building others up according to their needs, that it may benefit those who listen (Eph. 4:29)

Love Is Forgiving

There's no way you can give love without forgiveness. Forgiving your husband and giving him a second chance to prove himself is one of the greatest ways to show your husband love. Stop counting offenses or keeping records of all the things he did wrong. Without forgiveness, there's no love. You can't say you love your husband if you hold grievances against him. Sometimes, when I hear cases of unforgiveness in marriage conflicts, I ask God, "What has happened to our conscience?" The things that I hear most ladies hold as grievances against their husbands are minor issues. I heard a lady say she couldn't forgive her husband because he has never shown remorse or been remorseful! You may not agree with me here, but forgiveness is what you freely give to a person, without the person being apologetic for

> **FORGIVING YOUR HUSBAND AND GIVING HIM A SECOND CHANCE TO PROVE HIMSELF IS ONE OF THE GREATEST WAYS TO SHOW YOUR HUSBAND LOVE.**

what they did wrong. You forgive so you can free yourself. Saying you will never forgive your husband is like drinking poison and expecting your husband to die. Unforgiveness is a spiritual disease that if not dealt with immediately, dries up the love tank inside of you. And once you are that dry inside, it can lead to physical sickness. Many diagnoses have been linked to unforgiveness. Please be encouraged and start living the life of forgiveness with your husband. Someone sincerely asked me, "How many times do I have to keep forgiving?" Very interesting question. And I answered that question by simply reading the Bible, where one of the disciples (Peter) asked Jesus the same question. In case you also wonder about this, here's a reminder of what the Bible says about how many times we ought to forgive one another.

> Then Peter came to Jesus and asked, "Lord, how many times shall I forgive my brother or sister who sins against me? Up to seven times?" Jesus answered, "I tell you, not seven times, but seventy-seven times." (Matt. 18:21–22)

The interpretation of this scripture simply means you keep forgiving your husband as often as issues arise and if possible, forgive in advance. Indeed, love is forgiving.

Love Is Patient

Someone else might not really understand how you are feeling right now in your marriage or dealing with the ordeals you're passing through. But there is one sure thing: it takes patience to love. When you exercise patience with your husband, your love will never drain. When most ladies run out of patience, they take to nagging, which makes matters even worse. You can't speak of love without also mentioning how patient you are. It takes patience to love, and it takes love to be patient. Love and patience are compatible. When you practice these, you'll see positive results. We've heard many positive testimonies from couples we've counseled. You might be going through one

WHEN YOU EXERCISE PATIENCE WITH YOUR HUSBAND, YOUR LOVE WILL NEVER DRAIN.

issue or the other with your husband. No one will know or understand how painful it is for you, but hang in there, love him, and patiently wait until God touches his heart. We encourage ladies to be patient as long as the man is not violent; keep on loving him until he changes. Wives who gave positive testimonies practiced loving patiently. Apply this knowledge and you will surely see tremendous change.

> Be completely humble and gentle; be patient, bearing with one another in love. Make every effort to keep the unity of the Spirit through the bond of peace. (Eph. 4:2–3)

Love Is Tangible

God loved the world so much that He gave His only begotten Son, Jesus, to die for our sins. Nothing ascribes love as to be compared to the gift of salvation God gave to humanity. It is written in John 3:16: "For God so loved the world that he gave his one and only Son, that whoever believes in him shall not perish but have eternal life." Men also need gifts from their wives. Buying a gift for your husband cannot be ruled out as a way of showing love. It a myth that men don't appreciate gifts. Please, don't buy into that. It is true that we all have different love languages, but generally speaking, any type of man will appreciate a gift as proof of love. Gifts speak volumes about your love for your husband. So just as the Bible says faith without works is dead, know also that love without giving is dead. The amount spent on the gift is nothing compared to the love in the heart it came from. The motive for buying

THE MOTIVE FOR BUYING THE GIFT IS MORE IMPORTANT THAN THE GIFT ITSELF FOR ANY TYPE OF MAN.

the gift is more important than the gift itself for any type of man. Ladies, be encouraged to occasionally buy gifts for your husbands as proof of your love. Love is tangible.

Love Is Sex with Your Husband

This is an exclusive act of covenant in the relationship between you and your husband. Engage intimately with your husband and never deny him that. No love language speaks louder than when you make love with your man. Ladies, be encouraged to make the invitation from time to time. An invitation for sex must not always come from your husband. It should be mutual, and in general, men enjoy it more when the invitation comes from the wife. Do not buy into the myth that men should call for it because they are the ones who need it the most. Please, call for it, create the environment for it, and enjoy sex with your husband. Your invitation and preparation for sex with your husband speaks volume to him.

> May your kisses be as exciting as the best wine Yes, wine that goes down smoothly for my lover, flowing gently over lips and teeth. I am my lover's, and he claims me as his own. Come, my love, let us go out to the fields and spend the night among the wildflowers. Let us get up early and go to the vineyards to see if the grapevines have budded, if the blossoms have opened, and if the pomegranates have bloomed. There I will give you my love. There the mandrakes give off their fragrance, and the finest fruits are at our door, new delights as well as old, which I have saved for you, my lover. (Song of Sol. 7:9–13)

Things That Hinder Love
High Expectations: "Hope deferred makes the heart sick, but a longing fulfilled is a tree of life (Prov. 13:12)."

Nothing hinders love like having high expectations and hoping your husband will fulfill them, and then he fails. Many times, such expectations are based on what you know he's not naturally wired to do. They are not parts of his personality, but you desire them so much he becomes what you hoped for. If after living and bonding with him for years he's still not the complete person that you wished and hoped for, he may find it too difficult to become that person. It is then good enough to allow him to be who he is and enjoy your married life. If you continue to live with the expectation that one day he will become the person you so desire, it will only keep drying up your love tank.

Switch your expectations to those aspects of his personality where he *is* fulfilling your expectations in your marriage and be glad for those.

Your husband may not have it all, so focus on those boxes he does match and love him the more for who he is. At one of our counseling sessions, a wife was frustrated and complained bitterly that despite the number of years they had been married, she still had to remind her husband of her birthday. She said that it irritated her because every year she hoped he would remember but it got worse instead. The husband, on the other hand, was very apologetic and explained he did try his best but other things would distract him and then he would forget. (Was the husband's response a good enough reason to forget his wife's birthday? Perhaps not). Setting aside her husband forgetting her special day, I asked the wife if there was anything good her husband did in terms of showing love to her. She paused for a moment and then listed many positive things her husband did for her. She realized and agreed that her husband really was caring and loving to her.

> YOUR HUSBAND MAY NOT HAVE IT ALL, SO FOCUS ON THOSE BOXES HE DOES MATCH AND LOVE HIM THE MORE FOR WHO HE IS.

Bitterness: "Bear with each other and forgive one another if any of you has a grievance against someone. Forgive as the Lord forgave you. And over all these virtues put on love, which binds them all together in perfect unity (Col. 3:13–14)."

When you're holding grievances against your husband, you never can attain the level of loving him. As I write today, many couples are living together, but they are not talking to each other. Allowing or holding grievances has given rise to much bitterness in many marriages. Addressing it here, and again, I bring to your attention that forgiveness is a way of escape from whatever wrong you have endured from your husband. Know

> WHEN YOU'RE HOLDING GRIEVANCES AGAINST YOUR HUSBAND, YOU NEVER CAN ATTAIN THE LEVEL OF LOVING HIM.

that when you forgive, you love; and when you love, you are free internally. I have heard statements such as "Over my dead body will I forgive." Such statements should not be uttered in Christian homes. As believers, we're all products of forgiveness. God forgives us daily and expects us to forgive one another. Get rid of any malice towards your husband. Never allow whatever conflict you both have to linger. Take the lead by approaching him for resolution. For a marriage to thrive, I always say it takes just one person who understands the will of God to make it happen. If your husband doesn't get it, be the one that does get it. If he's in the wrong and not the least apologetic about it, don't act the same way he does. Two wrongs never make a right. There's nothing wrong with being angry at his attitude, but do not let that determine your own attitude. Do not hold malice for him; rather, go for reconciliation. "But now you must also rid yourselves of all such things as these: anger, rage, malice, slander, and filthy language from your lips (Col. 3:9)."

Wrong Foundations: "When the foundations are being destroyed, what can the righteous do (Ps. 11:3)?"

Some difficulties in marriages are experienced because love is not evident due to faulty foundations. The struggle you're having with loving your husband may be a result of your experiences growing up. A lady who grew up without experiencing love from her parents will have issues with giving love to the husband. Many women did not get love but instead abuse from their parents. People who experienced only an abusive relationship with their parents will have little to offer when they get married. A lady who grew up with an abusive father will likely fight against the husband on any little thing because it comes across as abusive to her.

> THE STRUGGLE YOU'RE HAVING WITH LOVING YOUR HUSBAND MAY BE A RESULT OF YOUR EXPERIENCES GROWING UP.

Such negative role models in one's childhood will have a huge impact when the person gets married. Getting to and dealing with the root of the issue is usually helpful. A husband kept getting accused of being unfaithful by the wife. When we got to the root, it was revealed that it was a result of the wife's father being unfaithful to her mother. Sometimes, due to their own bad experiences, mothers nurture their daughters to have the same perspective as they do, such as telling their daughters to never trust that any man will remain faithful in their marriage. This view is simply based on the mother's own experience from an unfaithful husband or father, and a wrong foundation is laid in a young girl's heart. If not broken, this wrong foundation can linger from one generation to the next. The daughter gets married and will never trust the husband, even if the man is innocent. The young woman's husband now pays the price for the generalized belief she got from her mom. Such a lady will eventually pass the same generalized belief to her own daughter, and her daughter to her own daughter, and it continues. Thus, this myth will remain in the family from generation to generation. This type of tale must be dealt with and must be broken so that love tanks can be filled enough to love husbands without measure.

Criticism: "So let's stop condemning each other. Decide instead to live in such a way that you will not cause another believer to stumble and fall (Rom. 14:13)."

When you focus on criticism and condemning your husband's personality or anything that he gets wrong, your love tank will definitely run dry. When a wife is always criticizing her husband for every little thing, she doesn't realize she's making things worse. Out of stubbornness, some men deliberately repeat those actions for which they are constantly being criticized by their wives, and this keeps the marriage troubled, without love flowing. I will not dwell here much so as to not repeat myself, but I would like to make it clear that there's nothing wrong with approaching your husband with anything you feel he does wrong, but do it with love, and sometimes ignore the little bits; don't reprimand him for everything you notice. Certain things are uncalled for, so just ignore them and move on. Learning to overlook certain things your husband does helps build your love tank.

CHAPTER 7

MAINTAINING YOUR BEAUTY

*How beautiful you are, my darling! Oh, how beautiful! Your eyes behind
your veil are doves. Your hair is like a flock of goats descending from the
hills of Gilead. Your teeth are like a flock of sheep just shorn, coming up
from the washing. Each has its twin; not one of them is alone. Your lips
are like a scarlet ribbon; your mouth is lovely. Your temples behind your
veil are like the halves of a pomegranate. Your neck is like the tower of
David, built with courses of stone; on it hang a thousand shields, all of
them shields of warriors. Your breasts are like two fawns, like twin fawns
of a gazelle that browse among the lilies. Until the day breaks and the
shadows flee, I will go to the mountain of myrrh and to the hill of incense.
You are altogether beautiful, my darling; there is no flaw in you.*
—Song of Solomon 4:1–7

It is very important to understand that your husband is attracted to your
beauty and will continually be entangled by that beauty. Your beauty
is the charm that bonds your husband to you. No other lady's beauty
can surpass your beauty in the eyes of your husband. There are certain
things about your beauty that attracted him the first time. Never allow
the devil to twist your mind into believing that you don't need to pay
attention to your looks anymore since you're already married. Ladies,
no matter what your age, please maintain your beautiful looks for your
husband. The beauty of a woman is in the eyes of the beholder.

Regardless of the aftereffects of childbearing, make efforts to maintain your beauty. You can never lose your beauty because you are fearfully and wonderfully made. But if you lose interest in maintaining your beauty, you lose it in the sight of your husband. Again, don't be deceived or confused, but understand that your beauty has nothing to do with your color, height, age, or size. Many ladies have berated themselves into low self-esteem because they believe they are no longer beautiful, having judged themselves by some of the criteria I've listed above.

> **NEVER ALLOW THE DEVIL TO TWIST YOUR MIND INTO BELIEVING THAT YOU DON'T NEED TO PAY ATTENTION TO YOUR LOOKS ANYMORE SINCE YOU'RE ALREADY MARRIED.**

Maintain the beauty you saw as a priority during those dating periods. Remember how important it was for you while you were dating or those days your fiancé planned on visiting? You would search your wardrobe for the most amazing dress to wear, handbags, and shoes to match. Don't forget the makeup you splashed on and styling your hair to ensure you looked fresh in his eyes. Those looks have not escaped your husband's memory. He's looking for that wife but may no longer be seeing her. I may not have scientific proof, but I can assure you that one of the root problems of an angry man is coming home to an unkempt wife. Nothing provokes a man like when the wife, after years of marriage, begins to care less for her looks. Physical attraction to a wife calms anxiety in a husband. That beauty of yours is the ego of your husband when he's out there in his spheres of influence.

It is never too late to get back to how you used to care for your beauty. Take good care of yourself for the primary purpose of remaining attractive to your husband. Your skin needs that soap and cream to keep it fresh, so go back to using them. Those lovely perfumes you usually wore during those dating periods, please wear them again. This might be one area you've not paid attention to lately, but I encourage you to make the effort and you'll see what happens.

Styling your hair or getting a manicure and pedicure as often as your budget can allow isn't bad at all. Maintaining your beauty not only captures the attention of your husband, but it brings self-fulfillment to you. This self-fulfillment brings satisfaction with how beautiful you are. When you're satisfied with your looks, you will want to maintain them. Don't be deceived or let your mind be twisted into believing that this is not needed after marriage. Maintaining your beauty is more necessary after marriage than ever before.

During the honeymoon, do you remember the nightclothes that made your husband want to grab you all the time? Where are those today? You need to understand that such memories need to be kept alive. A man is fulfilled if he is attracted to his wife at all times. Your physical appearance when he's at home with you or on an outing with you matters the most to him, more so than even how he himself looks.

Married life is not all about giving birth to kids and raising kids. As much as those are very vital in marriage, understand that it shouldn't make you lose focus on maintaining your beauty. Again, I must emphasize that maintaining your beauty has nothing to do with color, height, age, or size. Your husband is attracted to the way you look, either way. But I can assure you that your husband feels much better within himself when you maintain your beauty. Keep it up for him and never lose focus.

Myth

Wives, in the same way submit yourselves to your own husbands so that, if any of them do not believe the word, they may be won over without words by the behavior of their wives, when they see the purity and reverence of your lives. Your beauty should not come from outward adornment, such as elaborate hairstyles and the wearing of gold jewelry or fine clothes. Rather, it should be that of your inner self, the unfading beauty of a gentle and quiet spirit, which is of great worth in God's sight. For this is the way the holy women of the past who put their hope in God used to adorn themselves. They submitted themselves to their own husbands, like Sarah, who obeyed Abraham and called him her lord. You are her daughters if you do what is right and do not give way to fear. (1 Pet. 3:1–6)

This scripture has frequently been misinterpreted, causing many Christian wives to oppose the maintenance of outward beauty. Peter was actually addressing wives and their behaviors towards their husbands, which is true in our world today. If a woman maintains her outer beauty, practices all that's been discussed in this chapter on beauty, but is very disrespectful to the husband, her physical beauty will never keep him attracted to her. Men would rather live comfortably in peace with a wife who chooses to not care about her outer beauty but is respectful to him, than a wife who keeps her appearance spot on at all times but is very disrespectful. The scripture didn't condemn the maintenance of your physical beauty but instead emphasizes the importance of your character and how it matters most to your husband and people around you.

Some Christian denominations have adopted this scripture as the norm for how holy women should look. So, ladies who belong to such denominations believe holiness is in not paying attention to their looks. People in such denominations believe their ladies shouldn't wear earrings, dress well, or style or expose their hair. Ironically, separation and divorce are on the rise even in those denominations. This shows that something is not quite right somewhere. Neglecting your appearance as a wife and believing that to be holy is not biblical. When you walk in the Spirit and yield daily to the Holy Spirit, it helps you to walk in the Spirit and allows you to manifest the fruits of the Spirit. Manifesting the fruits of the Spirit makes you a holy woman. Your husband needs that the most and also needs to admire your beauty. Be wise and choose both. Maintain your beauty and holiness!

> I also want the women to dress modestly, with decency and propriety, adorning themselves, not with elaborate hairstyles or gold or pearls or expensive clothes, but with good deeds, appropriate for women who profess to worship God. (1 Tim. 2:9–10)

This scripture is addressing indecent dressing and is especially important in our generation today. That is why some weak men are falling into temptation, either looking lustfully or committing adultery. There are outfits designed to expose parts of your body that ought to be for your husband's eyes only. The scripture is telling women to refrain from wearing dresses that expose those parts of the body meant for their husbands' eyes only. However, wearing such dresses in your home is ideal and recommended for private display for your hubby in the bedroom. That is the real fun of maintaining your beauty. Wear those short skirts or dresses that show part of your body in your bedroom, but not outside. The scripture, which touches on hairstyles, gold, pearls, and expensive clothes, doesn't say they shouldn't be worn, but rather to wear them modestly. Just as a woman knows the appropriate outfit and hairstyle to wear for a job interview, the same goes for outfits to wear to a church service. For every outing, there's always an appropriate or suitable outfit and hairstyle that fits in. An outfit worn on a date with your husband will definitely be different from the one worn to work or church. The scripture is addressing inappropriate dressing, especially as we find in the church these days. Peter addressed this in his epistles, and Paul did as well is his letters to Timothy.

The scripture never condemns maintaining your beauty nor wearing good-looking outfits to match. It advises modesty and decent dressing among ladies. It also touches on applying wisdom to know what particular outfit fits in with a particular occasion. For example, church outfits should be extremely modest to avoid distracting others from worship.

Charm is deceptive, and beauty is fleeting; but a woman who fears the LORD is to be praised. (Prov. 31:30)

Beauty cannot be compared to a godly woman who fears the Lord. The husband is secure, her kids are in safe hands, and everyone around her is positively impacted. This is to say that caring for your outer beauty alone is not a prerequisite to positively impact the people around you. It takes efforts beyond maintaining a good appearance and outer beauty. Fear of God is the beginning of wisdom. Every man hopes and desires to be married to a godly wife who fears the Lord. Again, the scripture is not condemning beauty, nor is it saying that taking care of yourself is not needed. Those are needed, but being godly matters the most to your husband and kids, including the family/community where you found yourself.

Healthy Lifestyle: "Dear friend, I pray that you may enjoy good health and that all may go well with you, even as your soul is getting along well (3 John 1:2)."

Your husband is very much concerned about your health, beyond your outer beauty. Keeping up with your beauty is as good as maintaining good health. Maintaining good health requires a lot of discipline, which includes the kind of food you eat, exercise, and what you drink. Losing weight is a different issue, and eating good food that nourishes your body is another. No man wants to see his wife go down with ill health at any time. In most cases, men are more worried and concerned

> YOUR HUSBAND IS VERY MUCH CONCERNED ABOUT YOUR HEALTH, BEYOND YOUR OUTER BEAUTY.

about the health of their wives than they are about themselves. And when such worries set in, some wives start thinking the husband no longer loves them or self-pity kicks in. We've seen instances where couples go through difficulties over staying healthy. The husband feels the wife is neither eating healthy nor doing any kind of exercise.

One husband's frustration was because he was trying to live a healthy lifestyle, but the wife couldn't be bothered. Most of the time, they prepared separate meals due to different food choices. He said he had tried all possible ways to convince his wife to start paying attention to what she ate but failed. He acknowledged that forcing his wife would only worsen things, so he chose to keep encouraging her and even to start praying about it. On the wife's part, she said that all she got from her husband were constant reminders of the possible negative health effects from her choice of food, and that annoyed her a lot. Things like this should not cause conflict among couples, but they do. If you are one of those ladies, please understand that your husband means well and is concerned about your health and well-being. Many health issues today are a result of the things we eat. It is also very important to understand that as you age, taking extra care of your diet becomes very important. Receive this positively and be encouraged to maintain a healthy lifestyle

CHAPTER 8

COUNSELING

*Listen to advice and accept discipline, and at the
end you will be counted among the wise.*
—Proverbs 19:20

Many marriages are suffering, and most are already broken because couples lack knowledge. Knowledge is the key when it comes to living a happy married life. Those couples who are enjoying their marriages have acquired the knowledge needed for living a happily married life and are applying that knowledge. Nothing good comes by chance; it takes a lot of effort! Acquiring the necessary knowledge and applying it is key.

Often, we have men kick against marriage counseling because of their natural male ego. However, sometimes couples need counseling to attain and enjoy a quality married lifestyle. It is easy for a man to participate in any form of counseling, be it business matters or even healthy living, but when it comes to marriage, they shy away or struggle.

This chapter is simply to encourage and enlighten wives on the subject of counseling so they can encourage their husbands on its importance for marriages. For lack of knowledge, people perish. Ignorance has destroyed a lot of homes. I think it necessary to encourage you ladies to seek counseling and encourage your husbands to do the same.

The key word for discussing counseling with your husband is encouragement. Spend time encouraging him, choose your words wisely, and time what you say carefully. Pray for wisdom—God knows your husband more than you do. Do not operate under the assumption that he will not accept counseling. Nothing changes if you do nothing about what you want to see changed. Don't die in silence, or because of shame you endure your marriage, or worse, you choose to walk away. Marriage is meant to work and you're going to enjoy it if you know what to do and how to do it, by the grace of God.

> **PRAY FOR WISDOM—GOD KNOWS YOUR HUSBAND MORE THAN YOU DO.**

I met a lady who shared the story of her husband's drinking habit. She said she did her best to help her husband overcome the habit. Because the husband would not yield to a Christian counseling session, she decided to approach a secular group. She was so desperate to see him conquer the bad habit that she accompanied him daily as he received therapy. It was not an easy task for her, but she saw that she was the only motivator the husband needed to attain a normal life. It was a very painful and disturbing situation, but this lady vowed to pass the test. She's still married to the same man even as he's still undergoing therapy.

Another situation I'll like to share is the account of a conflict between a husband and wife that heated up to when the man lost his temper and physically abused the wife. The husband became so remorseful over his behavior that he apologized to the wife. This lady now used that opportunity to address an issue she had been longing to bring up. She had known her marriage would benefit from marriage counseling and had pressed and longed for it, but it wasn't forthcoming. That moment of her husband's error and remorsefulness became her opportunity, and she utilized it as the right time to introduce again, and passionately, the issue of going for counseling. The husband had no choice at that time but to agree to her suggestion. Today, they are still happily married and still going through marriage counseling, which is empowering their knowledge of marriage and family life.

I shared the above true-life stories to show that in most cases, if marital conflict is approached and dealt with appropriately, it can become a winning situation. Whichever method you can use to get your husband help, be it secular or Christian-based counseling, by all means please do use it.

> The words of the reckless pierce like swords, but the tongue of the wise brings healing. (Prov. 12:18)

Many men have turned their lives around for good due to their wives' counsel. And all of which depends on the wife's level of wisdom and her manner of approach. It is strongly recommended to first work with the husband to win victory in those areas that need change in your husband, instead of rushing into counseling on every issue. Although counseling is highly recommended, bear in mind that since men kick against it a lot, wisdom requires that you try your best to become your husband's mediator to counseling.

Your personal input about counseling can be a great help if you embark on measures to improve your marriage. Example of such measures includes reading good books on marriage. Getting mentorship from such books will help you share what you've learned with your husband. You can't give what you don't have. (So, if you are reading this book, well done—that's a good start!) If you read a book that deals with certain issues you know will benefit both of you, it becomes easier to introduce the book to your husband. Sharing the story and encouraging him to read the book can help solve so many issues that you might not need a counseling session. Any type of man will prefer to work by himself to become a better husband via a book you have introduced than to physically go to a counseling session.

When you see or hear of a book that will help him, buy that book, read it, and then pass it on to him. I am not advertising any book here, but I will recommend that any lady reading this book should also read my book *Not without the Head*. In that book, I challenge men to accept the role of loving unconditionally and share my personal struggles in my marriage. I learned things the hard way and struggled for a long time before the Holy Spirit gave birth to a new revelation in me that helped me out. It is highly recommended that men read such a book. Most men will not just pick up a book to read written by another man who they believe is airing a personal opinion. However, a wife can win him over by first reading the book and then personally introducing it to him. It will be easier for your husband to accept a book to read when you've read it. Such simple steps can infuse so much knowledge into your marriage, without you taking your husband to meet with a counselor.

The same goes for messages that are related to marriage and family. I'll recommend that wives introduce watching or listening to such messages with their husbands. Creating a special time for watching webinars or marriage seminars together might prevent a lot of havoc you could face in your marriage. I strongly believe that this new era of online seminars overrides any excuse any husband will give to their wives to avoid attending seminars that can help build up their marriage. Many good marriage counseling sessions are going on that do not even require the speakers or counselors to know who you are or if you attended. Search the internet; there are lots of websites, links, apps such as

CREATING A SPECIAL TIME FOR WATCHING WEBINARS OR MARRIAGE SEMINARS TOGETHER MIGHT PREVENT A LOT OF HAVOC YOU COULD FACE IN YOUR MARRIAGE.

YouTube, and you should look for seasoned and respected counselors with a good reputation for their counsel in any form, be it films, talks, books, or reports. Watch their counseling sessions together with your husband right there in your home.

Look for Zoom marriage conferences, register for such events, and encourage your husband to attend with you. I am not kidding you; this is the time to win the war of engaging your husband with counseling without dragging him out. Register for such programs and set a reminder for your husband. Those conferences are helpful, especially when the counselors are open to sharing their struggles and how they are overcoming them daily. Marriage issues will never stop, but handling them amicably when they do arise is the very wisdom needed for a happy marriage.

People sometimes relate to the personal stories these speakers or counselors tell. Hearing stories that relate to your own marriage or situation and how the issue was positively handled is a great asset, and if acquired and put to good use, will be beneficial to you and your husband.

Some webinars allow time for questions and answers, which most people find useful for addressing their own personal issues. Again, remember that nothing changes if nothing is done. Ask questions that affect your relationship the most. All things work together for good for those who love the Lord. If there's any good thing that has come out of the Covid-19 pandemic, it is a wide acceptance and use of online/virtual church services, conferences, seminars, etc. Utilize these when and where possible and available; they might work much better. Your husband might be more receptive to the virtual services rather than dragging him out to a venue for a marriage conference or counseling. Do not get me wrong; I still prefer physically onsite marriage conferences because of the bonding time it creates for couples, but the webinars, virtual conferences, and workshops available these days may work better, especially for those husbands who prefer to remain anonymous or want their privacy protected. Men love their privacy, and respecting this will help them yield to your requests, including going for counseling, marriage seminars, etc.

If you hear about any men's ministry that has a good track record and will benefit your husband, introduce that to him and allow him to make up his mind. Never assume that he will not be interested and ignore doing your own part. I've seen a lot of men attend conferences that they wouldn't normally have heard about unless their wives recommended them. Wives who truly appreciated how important it was for their husbands to fully understand their role in their marriages would research events that would help and recommended them to their husbands. Many positive testimonies are on record that show not only how the man became a better husband but also how he found his purpose just by attending such conferences. I know of a lady who recommended a particular conference to her husband, and at that conference the husband met Jesus as his Lord and personal Savior. The husband became born-again, a new man, a new husband, a better husband, and a new father to their kids. Today, that same man is a lead pastor, doing great things for the Lord with signs and wonders following his ministry. Show me a successful man, and I will show you a woman who refused to give up on that husband!

Individual Mentorship

In the same way, the women are to be worthy of respect, not malicious talkers but temperate and trustworthy in everything. (1 Tim. 3:11)

You must have that one person who you respect for the role she plays in her own marriage, and her successful marriage is worthy of emulation. Such a person, if found, could share helpful opinions with you and offer sound advice that can help in your own marriage, which can help you become better with your husband. A wife who has such a person as a mentor can open up and share issues that she's struggling within her marriage and receive counsel. Such counseling should be between you and your mentor only. I prefer and highly recommend that such a mentor be a fellow lady who has a good track record in her marriage. However, make sure your husband knows of this mentor. Remember, nothing is to be hidden in your marriage. Let your husband know about your mentor, but not necessarily letting him know about your counseling with her except as you choose to. Open up to your mentor, and never be ashamed of asking for help with your personal struggles.

Sharing your marriage struggles with a trusted mentor will enable you to get counsel that can help you become better in your approaches with your husband, which will, in turn, change your husband. Also, having a trusted mentor who can weigh your opinions before you act goes a long way as well. There might be things you may consider as the best approach for a conflict resolution, but after a counseling session with your mentor, you might just realize your intended action is not worth it, or it might appear you need a different approach. Little processes like this have been neglected among married couples. It takes knowledge to build a happy married life, so acquire it as often as possible. The more you know, the better wife you'll become, and a changed and better husband you'll have.

Sisters' Fellowship and Mentorship

You, however, must teach what is appropriate to sound doctrine. Teach the older men to be temperate, worthy of respect, self-controlled, and sound in faith, in love and in endurance. Likewise, teach the older women to be reverent in the way they live, not to be slanderers or addicted to much wine, but to teach what is good. Then they can urge the younger women to love their husbands and children, to be self-controlled and pure, to be busy at home, to be kind, and to be subject to their husbands, so that no one will malign the word of God. (Titus 2:1–5)

Just as I challenged men to be under mentorship with other godly men who will teach and mentor them on becoming good husbands and fathers, the same goes for ladies. I encourage ladies to belong to a godly sisters' fellowship, where you can be taught by the elderly ones among you about being a virtuous wife. Mentorship helps because you learn from people older than you or who might have been through all that you're experiencing. With their experiences and knowledge, these women are in the position to give you godly counsel. Such a relationship is ideal, especially for the newly married couples out there. When you're guided and taught well, guess what? Your life will begin to minister to your husband. No counsel is a greater teacher to a man than the actions of a woman who learns that patience wins the race in marriage, and she begins to practice having patience with the husband. If such a wife is known for her impatience but makes a turnaround through mentorship programs, her new self will not go unnoticed by the husband, and he'll be left with no choice but to blend with the new rhythm.

Friends' Mentorship

Walk with the wise and become wise, for a companion of fools suffers harm. (Prov. 13:20)

A mentorship program gives you the opportunity to associate with the wise. Having fellowship with sisters who have good fruits in their marriages will help you learn what they know, and you may get the same result. Although divorce is very common these days, that doesn't make it the best or the only way out. God is still in the business of restoring homes. There are many issues and reasons why divorce happens, but we're not going to dwell on all of it here. What I'd like to add, though, is that the type of people with whom you surround yourself makes a huge difference to your life. If you have many friends who are divorcees and who couldn't care less about marriage and thus live a wayward lifestyle, the tendency is that you'll be heading towards divorce, knowingly or unknowingly. Such relationships are not healthy for your marriage; rather they could destroy it. Disconnect from such relationships. Instead, have fellowship with friends who have good intentions and can impact your husband positively.

> THE TYPE OF PEOPLE WITH WHOM YOU SURROUND YOURSELF MAKES A HUGE DIFFERENCE TO YOUR LIFE.

Mother's Mentorship

Even when I am old and gray, do not forsake me, my God, till I declare your power to the next generation, your mighty acts to all who are to come. (Ps. 71:18)

Do not neglect good counsel from your mom or mother-in-law; however, be sensitive and alert so you do not miss the chance to seek out marriages with good track records. This could even be with a repentant parent who is willing to teach you the truth from the mistakes they've made in their own marriages. Such counsel will help your journey towards enjoying your marriage. No other person can tell you the truth more than your own parents. When a mom opens up about her past mistakes, it transforms you positively. A good mom will never stand back and watch her daughter make the same mistakes she made in her own early years of marriage. Listen to the counsel of such dear moms to enjoy your marriage. Remember, you can't change your husband, but you can change yourself. And when you change yourself through the godly counsels of moms, your husband will change for good.

Marriage Mentorship

The proverbs of Solomon son of David, king of Israel: for gaining wisdom and instruction; for understanding words of insight; for receiving instruction in prudent behavior, doing what is right and just and fair; for giving prudence to those who are simple, knowledge and discretion to the young—let the wise listen and add to their learning, and let the discerning get guidance—for understanding proverbs and parables, the sayings and riddles of the wise. The fear of the LORD is the beginning of knowledge, but fools despise wisdom and instruction. (Prov. 1:1–7)

Marriage mentorship is one area where you need wisdom and prayers to get your husband to buy into the idea. It's easier when the husband understands the power in marriage mentorship than when a wife is the one that has the understanding. Either way, never give up on trying your best to make your husband understand the importance of marriage mentorship. Marriage mentorship builds accountability from mentees to their mentors. The people you engage in this type of marriage mentorship should be couples with good track records in their own marriages. These couples, like your individual mentors, will be transparent about their marriage experiences with you and your husband. It's really important to choose mentors from people ahead of you and your husband in both age and time spent as married couples. Their experiences cannot be bought with money. When couples have such a mentorship relationship introduced to their marriage, it builds good accountability among couples and opportunities to ask questions or help resolve disputes for the mentees.

Marriage mentorship can include regular or irregular meetings depending on what couples choose. A mentorship relationship is far easier to build than counseling because there is no conflict waiting to be resolved at the very start of it. Most mentorship meetings are informal; some are based purely on questions and answers relative to married life experiences or addressing issues around decision-making among couples. You will gain a lot by engaging and submitting to these mentors who are ahead of you in their own marriages. I must remind you that there is nothing impossible with God; never underestimate what the Lord can and will do. Talk to your husband about marriage mentorship and the importance of it, and if possible, allow him to lead on choosing your marriage mentor.

Marriage Counseling

> For lack of guidance a nation falls, but victory is won through many advisers. (Prov. 11:14)

Marriage counseling must be introduced when things remain the same, even after you have sincerely worked on improving yourself and have made all necessary sacrifices to ensure your marriage works. As much as men kick against counseling, you shouldn't allow yourself to be driven through the wall because you are both trying to figure it all on your own. Marriage counseling has saved a lot of broken homes and is still on top of the game to this day. If you've improved yourself through the methods we have discussed earlier, including mentorship programs, and you're seeing no change in your husband, then you need to seek help from trained, qualified, or autonomous marriage counselors. Again, it takes wisdom and prayers to have your husband know about your intentions. Respect his headship, and never share anything with anyone without his consent. Seek his consent, let him know how you're feeling, and why it is necessary that both of you see a counselor. Soft and seasoned words of encouragement will surely make your husband yield to your request. In most cases, men seem to not be serious when they go with you to

SOFT AND SEASONED WORDS OF ENCOURAGEMENT WILL SURELY MAKE YOUR HUSBAND YIELD TO YOUR REQUEST.

meet a counselor. Never let his attitude discourage you. Stick to the counsel, and it will save your marriage. And as I mentioned earlier, it doesn't really matter whether it is secular or Christian counseling. Just go for counseling when things are getting out of hand. I do recommend Christian counseling, especially for couples who are believers, but I do not despise secular counseling.

Marriage Abuse

I said, "I will watch my ways and keep my tongue from sin; I will put a muzzle on my mouth while in the presence of the wicked." So I remained utterly silent, not even saying anything good. But my anguish increased; my heart grew hot within me. While I meditated, the fire burned; then I spoke with my tongue: "Show me, LORD, my life's end and the number of my days; let me know how fleeting my life is. You have made my days a mere handbreadth; the span of my years is as nothing before you. Everyone is but a breath, even those who seem secure. Surely everyone goes around like a mere phantom; in vain they rush about, heaping up wealth without knowing whose it will finally be. But now, Lord, what do I look for? My hope is in you. Save me from all my transgressions; do not make me the scorn of fools. I was silent; I would not open my mouth, for you are the one who has done this. Remove your scourge from me; I am overcome by the blow of your hand. When you rebuke and discipline anyone for their sin, you consume their wealth like a moth— surely everyone is but a breath. Hear my prayer, LORD, listen to my cry for help; do not be deaf to my weeping. I dwell with you as a foreigner, a stranger, as all my ancestors were. Look away from me, that I may enjoy life again before I depart and am no more." (Ps. 39:1–13)

Permit me to bring up abuse again to this chapter. If I had my way, I would bring it up in all the chapters. Almost everything we've discussed so far in this book, has been through abuse in one way or the other. In the discussion about counseling, you see abuse when the man refuses to go counseling, and yet things in the marriage are not working out fine. It is one thing for him to behave himself and try to do all that is expected of him, so his wife can live peacefully with him. But he just refuses counseling, so my advice would be for you to respect his opinion and be submissive to his headship. However, if things get worse and your plea for counseling is rejected by him, please do not die in silence. It is a sure sign of abuse, and I then would recommend that you let him know your intention of alerting a counselor. Pray for God's guidance to choose the right counselor, one who can approach him, but you need to seek a counselor when things become unbearable. Don't hide under the shadow of abusiveness in the name of submission. It is not right and shouldn't be encouraged.

Many ladies tolerate abuse in their marriage because they mistake their silence for being submissive, but for me, it is a clear case of abuse and should not be accepted anywhere. I usually advise wives to not condone any kind of physical abuse from any man. Although the first time can be considered a mistake, but the second time is no longer a mistake and must be reported—and such situations call for counseling. Never keep silent if you're in an abusive relationship. You're not helping him, and you are not helping yourself. We've witnessed such unexposed cases, and when they finally came to light, either the lady has dried up emotionally, causing depression and even physical illness, or there is an outburst and a request for divorce from the lady because she can't endure things any longer. It is better to seek counseling than to die in silence.

CHAPTER 9

PRAYERS

*Then Jesus told his disciples a parable to show them
that they should always pray and not give up.*
—Luke 18:1

"I am tired, I have done everything I could possibly do, yet things are not working. The man I used to love is no longer the man that I am living with. I can't handle it anymore. I have done all that I have been asked to do, yet it's still not working out. I am done with this marriage, and nothing can change my mind."

We hear a lot of these statements of frustration from many disappointed ladies who feel they have done their best to save their marriages. You might have felt or still feel the same as the lady I described. I do empathize with you. Please permit me to say that there is one vital thing you cannot give up on, and that is praying to the Lord, who is the author and finisher of your faith. Prayers have done wonders and yield positive results for those who didn't give up on them. One thing for sure is that prayers work. God answers our prayers. When He will answer or how He will answer is the mystery behind prayers.

> ONE THING FOR SURE IS THAT PRAYERS WORK. GOD ANSWERS OUR PRAYERS.

People give up easily because the answer to their prayers is not as timely as they desire. God's ways and our ways are never the same; neither are our thoughts and His thoughts the same. His will shall be done and not our will. Your prayers might be for God to change your husband, but the Holy Spirit could be saying that you're the one who needs to be changed.

Thanksgiving

Devote yourselves to prayer, being watchful and thankful. (Col. 4:2)

Change the pattern of your prayers. Instead of going straight into lamentation, try to first devote time thanking God for your husband. I keep saying that no matter how bad you think your spouse is, there are many areas where he's good. Thank God for those areas, thank God for life, and thank God for everything. Again, know that no matter how bad your spouse is, he is better than many other men out there. Starting your prayers with thanksgiving clears the mind and the burden of whatever weight you carry. Thanksgiving makes a pathway of clearer communication with God. It lightens the heart and allows every anger or bitterness to clear away. If you're upset and you find yourself lamenting to God in your prayers, you can only hear yourself and will not be able to hear God. Anger and bitterness block the flow of communication when we pray. Thanksgiving ushers you into the presence of God Most High. Thank God for who your husband is, and you will begin to appreciate your husband all the more. It changes your mindset, how you view your husband, and the kind of things you harbor in your heart concerning him. Rather than focusing on his weaknesses, reflect on his strengths, and begin to thank God for your husband and appreciate him. Thanksgiving is being grateful to God.

Sincerity

Who can understand his errors? Cleans thou me from secret faults. Keep back thy servant also from presumptuous sins; let them not have dominion over me: then shall I be upright, and I shall be innocent from the great transgression. Let the words of my mouth,

and the meditation of my heart, be acceptable in thy sight, O
LORD, my strength, and my redeemer. (Ps. 19:12–14, KJV)

Present your concerns and the issues you have with your husband
to God in prayers with all sincerity. Ask God to open your eyes to see
if there are any errors in you. Many conflicts are unresolved because
everyone involved sees themselves or their action as the right thing to
do. If you enter into prayers with all sincerity and ask God to reveal to
you anything wrong in your actions or what you've said, then surely
the Holy Spirit will minister to you. Perform a self-check to see if you
were arrogant or used harsh words when you were trying to express
yourself to your spouse. If that happened, you must ask God to forgive
you, and God will definitely forgive, and you will feel the forgiveness
of God right away. The weight of anger or resentment you feel towards
your husband will begin to fade away. You will feel lighter and willing
to resolve the conflict with your husband. This works even better than
involving a third party to resolve issues with your spouse. Humans are
easily offended, especially when they hear the opposite of what they
want or expect to hear. Many have walked away from counseling sessions to become even worse than they were before they started. Why?
Because they were told what they didn't want to hear. But when you
enter into prayers with sincerity, asking God to reveal to you if there are
any faults in you or presumptuous sins, He will reveal these to you, and
you will receive them clearly and understand it better than someone else
telling you. It is also a great privilege because right there in the prayer
mood, you're asking God for forgiveness for the mistakes you've made
or are still making in your relationship with your husband.

Listening

I will listen to what God the LORD says; he promises peace to
his people, his faithful servants but let them not turn to folly.
(Ps. 85:8)

Just as you enter into your prayer closet in sincerity, also practice
being still so you can hear what the Lord has to say to you. There might

be many conflicting issues going on between you and your husband, and you can't understand where they are coming from. These issues can even be draining you emotionally. Just enter into your prayer closet, lie down in whichever position you feel comfortable, and be still so God can speak to you. God already knows what has happened and why you have come to His presence, so even without you lamenting or uttering a word, the Holy Spirit is ever present, ready to speak to you. Listening is one vital prayer connection that many believers are missing. Those who practice listening, hear God speak concerning issues at hand, the ones that are yet to come, and of course, the wisdom and grace to navigate through them as they come.

> **THOSE WHO PRACTICE LISTENING, HEAR GOD SPEAK CONCERNING ISSUES AT HAND, THE ONES THAT ARE YET TO COME, AND OF COURSE, THE WISDOM AND GRACE TO NAVIGATE THROUGH THEM AS THEY COME.**

Intercession

But I tell you, love your enemies and pray for those who persecute you, that you may be children of your Father in heaven. He causes his sun to rise on the evil and the good, and sends rain on the righteous and the unrighteous. If you love those who love you, what reward will you get? Are not even the tax collectors doing that? And if you greet only your own people, what are you doing more than others? Do not even pagans do that? Be perfect, therefore, as your heavenly Father is perfect. (Matt. 5:44–48)

When you learn to pray for your husband regardless of how you feel or whatever you feel he's doing that is hurting you most, the change you anticipate will surely happen. God expects you to pray for him. Who knows if it is your prayers that will deliver him? There are many positive testimonies of men who were nonbelievers but repented because of a prayerful woman who refused to give up. Pray your husband into that man you desire to have as a husband. Never focus on the ugly things that he does that trigger sad emotions. Instead, enter your prayer closet and keep praying for him. Many wives allow squabbles with their husbands to push them into not praying for their husbands, and this causes things to get even worse. Praying for your husband works and should be encouraged. Never, for any reason, tag your husband as your enemy. And even if that thought sets in, the Word of the Lord demands you pray for your enemy. Pray for your husband; he is not your enemy, even when you feel so—pray for him because the Word of the Lord says so. Pray for those areas of his weaknesses that you want him to change. Remember, you can't change him, but God can. Intercede for him; ask for mercy and forgiveness on his behalf. Pray that God touches his heart to repent on those things you want to see changed. Bless his career, business, or ministry. Wish him well and keep believing that God will definitely turn things around for good. If there is one thing you should not give up in your marriage, it is consistent intercession for your husband.

Prayer Partner

Truly I tell you, whatever you bind on earth will be bound in heaven, and whatever you loose on earth will be] loosed in heaven. "Again, truly I tell you that if two of you on earth agree about anything they ask for, it will be done for them by my Father in heaven. For where two or three gather in my name, there am I with them." (Matt. 18:18–20)

Praying with your husband resolves conflicts faster than you may think. Couples that pray together have fewer conflicts than couples who don't pray together. Have your conflicts resolved in prayer and practice praying with your husband. There's nothing wrong with having a prayer partner, but the best prayer partner you could have is your spouse. The devil understands the power of agreement prayers when couples pray together, and that is

COUPLES THAT PRAY TOGETHER HAVE FEWER CONFLICTS THAN COUPLES WHO DON'T PRAY TOGETHER.

why he's constantly causing division among couples so they don't pray together. The devil has devised means of keeping couples from praying together. Some of these tricks show up as inflicting conflicts, having very busy and tight schedules, tiredness, forgetfulness, nonchalant attitude towards praying together, and lots of other distractions. Just be encouraged as you read this book, and be reminded that there is power behind agreement prayers with your husband. Never stop praying together with your husband. If your husband is weak in prayer, encourage him to start fulfilling his priesthood duties, which consist of praying constantly with you.

Like I said earlier, there's nothing wrong with confiding in a trusted friend who becomes your prayer partner. There's power behind agreement prayers. If you are struggling or not comfortable with having your husband as a prayer partner on any issue because of how he will feel about it and you have a trusted friend to pray with, please do so as there's nothing wrong with it. Just be careful and make sure that such a person can be trusted to keep your prayer points within the circle in which you share them. We've witnessed many occasions when information was leaked out because an issue was raised as a prayer point within a circle of so-called prayer partners. Again, make sure your husband is aware of your prayer partner. He will not be interested in knowing your prayer points, but he will be interested in knowing who that person is. Never conceal who your prayer partner is from your husband. Tell him ahead of time and do not make him find out on his own. It usually defeats the good intention when the man finds out that you have a prayer partner that he's not aware of. (Wives, please place great emphasis on having a female as your prayer partner.)

Corporate Prayer

When they heard this, they raised their voices together in prayer to God. "Sovereign Lord," they said, "you made the heavens and the earth and the sea, and everything in them. You spoke by the Holy Spirit through the mouth of your servant, our father David: "Why do the nations rage and the peoples plot in vain? The kings of the earth rise up and the rulers band together against the Lord and against his anointed one. Indeed Herod and Pontius Pilate met together with the Gentiles and the people of Israel in this city to conspire against your holy servant Jesus, whom you anointed. They did what your power and will had decided beforehand should happen. Now, Lord, consider their threats and enable your servants to speak your word with great boldness. Stretch out your hand to heal and perform signs and wonders through the name of your holy servant Jesus." After they prayed, the place where they were meeting was shaken. And they were all filled with the Holy Spirit and spoke the word of God boldly. (Acts 4:24-31)

There's power when believers gather together to pray. Many examples are recorded in the Bible when believers gathered together to pray and God answered them immediately. There can be certain issues concerning your husband that might require you to enter into a corporate prayer. Most churches organize marriage seminars and special prayers for families. Never miss these events simply because you feel it wouldn't make any difference. Your personal prayers or prayers with your praying partner have their own impact, and when believers gather to pray, it has a different impact. I'll strongly advise you to prioritize accordingly—taking your personal prayer altar first, then your prayer partner's, and lastly the corporate prayers. Corporate prayers are ideal for general problems, such as sickness, barrenness, loss of job, etc. Corporate prayers are not usually for resolving conflicts, but it can be done wisely if you write your petition and put it into the prayer box without mentioning names. God, who sees every secret, will honor your heart's desire when believers are gathered together in one accord for prayers.

Prophetic Utterance

And they rose early in the morning and went out into the wilderness of Tekoa. And when they went out, Jehoshaphat stood and said, "Hear me, Judah and inhabitants of Jerusalem! Believe in the LORD your God, and you will be established; believe his prophets, and you will succeed. (2 Chron. 20:20)

Believe in the prophetic utterances of a spiritual father, usually your pastor. Many are under the cover of the grace upon the lives of their pastors without taking advantage of it. It is absolutely appropriate to ask your pastor to pray for your marriage. In most instances, pastors don't need you to explain the details of what's going on in your marriage but can give prophetic utterances that will begin to touch the areas of your concern. Believe that a pastor who is genuine and walks in the Spirit might begin to utter words of counseling, even in prayer, without knowing that it is impacting you directly. Believe those words of prayers and run with them. Most times, pastors prepare their sermons for the day without knowing whom the sermon will impact directly. Never be disobedient when such comes your way. Like I said earlier, abuse of Christian belief is everywhere, so it's no surprise that we have many false prophets who have done more harm than good. That should not make the true prophet a liar. The gifts of God are real, and there are still many who carry such gifts and utilize them well. Never shy away from asking your pastor to pray for your marriage. Should your pastor inquire about the details of what's going on, tell the pastor, as there's nothing wrong with that, but make sure you let your husband know before sharing.

CHAPTER 10

LIVING OUT YOUR RESPONSIBILITIES

Oh, how I love your law! I meditate on it all day long. Your commands are always with me and make me wiser than my enemies. I have more insight than all my teachers, for I meditate on your statutes. I have more understanding than the elders, for I obey your precepts. I have kept my feet from every evil path so that I might obey your word. I have not departed from your laws, for you yourself have taught me. How sweet are your words to my taste, sweeter than honey to my mouth! I gain understanding from your precepts; therefore I hate every wrong path.
—Psalm 119:97–104

Steven (not his real name) and his wife connected with me for counseling a few months ago. He reached out to me recently, while I was starting to write this book, so I felt it proper to introduce my discussion with him in this chapter. He made contact to let me know he had overcome the temptation of physically abusing his wife. The physical abuse of his wife was mainly prompted by her use of harsh words with him, but this time around, he didn't succumb to that temptation, because he applied all he had been learning in counseling. Nothing fulfills our marital rites like each couple fulfilling their own responsibilities, especially after acquiring the knowledge needed to have a successful married life.

It gladdened my heart to hear Steven's testimony and how he had started to apply all he's been learning from counseling to his marriage.

During their counseling session, Steven actually admitted he hated his rash behavior towards his wife. We advised the wife to forgive him, especially as he was open and willing to get the help necessary to change, including taking the bold step to get counseling.

Additionally, I encouraged his wife to work on herself to avoid using harsh words with her husband. I advised her that Steven is the absorbing type of man. Although he was very quiet and doesn't appear like the type that would ever raise his hands against his wife, this type of man falls victim to being physically abusive as the only means of fighting back for their headship. The wife accepted the advice to forgive but insisted she wouldn't tolerate any more physical abuse ever again from Steven. I totally agreed with her but also empathized with Steven, so I promised that I would work alongside him to achieve change.

I observed that the wife was more interested in us sorting out the husband's issue with physical abuse than she was in us finding and addressing what usually led to the physical abuse. There's a popular saying that there's no smoke without fire." As much as I will always condemn any form of abuse, be it verbal or physical, by men on their wives, I will always encourage wives to also work on themselves, and to try to refrain from those things that provoke their men to fight back wrongly.

Now back to Steven again. He mentioned he had to walk away for some fresh air when his wife was verbally abusing him, just like we advised him during the counseling session. He said, "My wife's harsh words were killing me but that day, I remembered your counsel and I quietly walked away for fresh air." Later that day, he initiated reconciliation with his wife, and they resolved their differences.

Why did I bring this story here? It takes one person who seeks and acquires the knowledge necessary to make a marriage work. I respect the opinion of other counselors who believe and teach that it takes two for marriage to work, but I believe it can take just one person to make it work. Using the story of Steven, I observed that on the day I counseled them, the wife wasn't concerned about her own weakness but was very concerned about the husband's weakness. You can imagine what could have happened on that fateful day if Steven didn't choose to walk away or wasn't determined to keep his end of the bargain by focusing on working out his weakness. He chose to apply the simple tactic he learned from counseling. He not only walked away for fresh air but came back and still showed his wife unconditional love. Regardless of who was wrong or right, he chose to apply what he learned by not allowing conflict to linger on unnecessarily. Conflicts are inevitable, but how you resolve them when they arise is all that matters.

> **I RESPECT THE OPINION OF OTHER COUNSELORS WHO BELIEVE AND TEACH THAT IT TAKES TWO FOR MARRIAGE TO WORK, BUT I BELIEVE IT CAN TAKE JUST ONE PERSON TO MAKE IT WORK.**

Just as men should focus on the responsibility of loving their wives unconditionally, this book is a great opportunity to encourage all ladies out there to focus on their own responsibility of respecting their husbands.

Do not merely listen to the word, and so deceive yourselves. Do what it says. Anyone who listens to the word but does not do what it says is like someone who looks at his face in a mirror and, after looking at himself, goes away and immediately forgets what he looks like. But whoever looks intently into the perfect law that gives freedom, and continues in it—not forgetting what they have heard, but doing it—they will be blessed in what they do. (Prov. 1:22–25)

I have done my best to lay out all that I think any type of man is seeking from his wife. I might be wrong on certain things I've written or naïve about certain things, but the fact is that if you've read this book this far and you're sincere with yourself, you have agreed with my narrative in the areas where they might have made sense to you. I beseech you to begin to apply them in your marriage and see your husband become a new person. Believe me, it works like magic. Once you focus on your own responsibility and ignore your husband's responsibility, you'll begin to perfect those areas of your weaknesses. Have enough of fighting for your rights and begin to live up to your responsibilities. The more you fulfill your responsibilities, the better your husband will become at his, and this makes a successful marriage.

Do nothing out of selfish ambition or vain conceit. Rather, in humility value others above yourselves, not looking to your own interests but each of you to the interests of the others. (Phil. 2:3–4)

When you make the choice to bring to your life all that you've learned so far, you will automatically begin to think first of your husband's interest more than yours. Going back to the story of Steven and his wife—if the wife begins to focus on working to overcome her own weakness, it will bring about tremendous change to her situation. I agree that Steven's physical abusiveness towards her is totally wrong and shouldn't be tolerated, but if she would try not using harsh words or being verbally abusive, Steven would have nothing to react to. On the contrary, Steven practiced the scripture (Phil. 2:3–4) quoted above when he walked away for fresh air and later came back to reconcile with her. At that moment, Steven wasn't interested in how he felt from those harsh words that came from his wife. rather, he focused on looking out for his wife's best interest at that moment.

Virtuous Woman

A wife of noble character who can find? She is worth far more than rubies. Her husband has full confidence in her and lacks nothing of value. She brings him good, not harm, all the days of her life. She selects wool and flax and works with eager hands. She is like the merchant ships, bringing her food from afar. She gets up while it is still night; she provides food for her family and portions for her female servants. She considers a field and buys it; out of her earnings she plants a vineyard. She sets about her work vigorously; her arms are strong for her tasks. She sees that her trading is profitable, and her lamp does not go out at night. In her hand she holds the distaff and grasps the spindle with her fingers. She opens her arms to the poor and extends her hands to the needy. When it snows, she has no fear for her household; for all of them are clothed in scarlet. She makes coverings for her bed;

she is clothed in fine linen and purple. Her husband is respected at the city gate, where he takes his seat among the elders of the land. She makes linen garments and sells them, and supplies the merchants with sashes. She is clothed with strength and dignity; she can laugh at the days to come. She speaks with wisdom, and faithful instruction is on her tongue. She watches over the affairs of her household and does not eat the bread of idleness. Her children arise and call her blessed; her husband also, and he praises her: "Many women do noble things, but you surpass them all." Charm is deceptive, and beauty is fleeting; but a woman who fears the LORD is to be praised. Honor her for all that her hands have done, and let her works bring her praise at the city gate. (Prov. 31:10–31)

I included this scripture in chapter 3 of this book, and I am reposting it here to emphasize that living out your responsibilities as a wife is the summary of being a virtuous woman. Being that virtuous woman is attainable simply by living out your responsibilities. Let this book inspire you to begin living out all you've read, heard, and learned. At times, we know exactly what is expected of us, but we choose to do otherwise. Be among those women who choose to live out their responsibilities regardless of their husbands' weaknesses. Set good examples and become a role model. That is what being a virtuous woman is all about.

> **LIVING OUT YOUR RESPONSIBILITIES AS A WIFE IS THE SUMMARY OF BEING A VIRTUOUS WOMAN.**

Impact of a Virtuous Woman

Husband: "A wife of noble character is her husband's crown, but a disgraceful wife is like decay in his bones (Prov. 12:4)."

When you begin to live out your responsibilities in your marriage, your husband feels the impact all the more. He becomes proud of you, boasts about his wife, and guess what? He will love you unconditionally. Nothing can be compared to a woman living out her responsibilities. Show me a successful man, and I will show you a virtuous wife beside him. It is priceless, and nothing can be compared to a virtuous woman married to any type of man. "She is more precious than rubies; nothing you desire can compare with her (Prov. 3:15)." Choose to impact your husband's life by practicing all that you've learned

Kids: "Her children arise and call her blessed (Prov. 31:28a)."

Apart from your husband, your kids are also being impacted. The legacy you leave behind matters a lot in their lives. Kids learn faster from what they see than from what you tell them. You can imagine what will happen if you keep using harsh words towards their dad, and then turn around and try to teach them about respect. If kids see the opposite of what you are teaching them, they grow up being very rebellious, especially among the believers. You can pray all you want or quote the Bible as often as possible, but when you are disrespectful and use harsh words with their dad, all you say becomes meaningless to them. Be encouraged to live out your responsibility and pass a good legacy to your kids. Becoming a virtuous woman is attainable.

Community: "The LORD bless you, my daughter," he replied. "This kindness is greater than that which you showed earlier: You have not run after the younger men, whether rich or poor. And now, my daughter, don't be afraid. I will do for you all you ask. All the people of my town know that you are a woman of noble character (Ruth 3:10–11)."

People around you will benefit when you live out your responsibilities in your marriage. Not only will your husband and children be impacted, but also the community. Everyone will notice your noble character because it is tangible. Younger ones will like to associate with you and learn from you. People will say good things about you, wherever you find yourself in the community you live in. You will always leave a legacy of good character behind, and such is expected of you when you choose to be a virtuous woman

Now that you have read about living out your responsibilities and their impact, I will encourage you to also begin to do everything in your capacity to encourage other women by educating them on what you know and are practicing. Together, we shall restore broken homes. Be a mentor to your kids or younger ladies who are newly married. Have them read more books, and encourage them to listen to audio programs that will help them live a stress-free married life. Many get into marriage without any knowledge of what marriage is really all about. It is time for you to not just live out your responsibility but also mentor others.

Living Together and Not Being Married: This is on the increase now—a man and a woman living together and making babies. They address themselves as boyfriend and girlfriend. This is not God's plan from the beginning of creation. That it has become acceptable these days does not make it proper. I'm therefore seizing this opportunity to challenge all virtuous women out there to help mentor young ladies and educate them well on the purpose of marriage. Many have chosen the route of boyfriend/girlfriend because many broken homes exist these days—too many. Some get into marriage with the preconception that if it doesn't work, they'll just go their separate ways without hesitation or second thoughts. These decisions made by two grown adults are choices that are negatively affecting or impacting the kids. The pain falls on the children who find themselves in such circumstances. Marriage is good and enjoyable when we know what to do and then do those things. It's fun and loveable. Marriage is an institution ordained by God. Many are missing this understanding today because they search for teachings and seek understanding of marriage from the wrong sources. If we want a successful marriage, we must return to the original source. God is the creator and initiator of marriage. Virtuous women should enlighten others about this sacred institution, just as the men are challenged to take on their headship mandate in homes.

Single by Choice: Being single is another choice that is becoming very popular. There are a lot of single moms out there by choice and their own decision. Such is neither biblical nor proper. I am not talking about those that became single moms based on the loss of their husband or due to terrible issues that eventually led to divorce, or those who chose to remain celibate. I am addressing those women who have chosen to remain unmarried while making babies with different men. Such acts need to be addressed and corrected. Let the women of noble character, who understand their responsibilities in a marriage and are living it, begin to positively influence these single-by-choice mothers. By living an exemplary married lifestyle, these women will encourage the original purpose of marriage, and broken homes shall be restored in Jesus's name. Amen

Don't ever feel condemned but become convinced to repent from any wrongdoing or bad behavior you've found yourself in, whether you are married or unmarried. What matters most is have a heart willing to do the right thing. There is no sin that cannot be forgiven. All that matters is repentance and moving forward. Your future is greater than the present.

In Conclusion: Let this book serve as a guide and an insight that will help you understand your husband and help mold you into becoming a role model for others. Start living all that resonates with you from reading this book, as it will help reduce the statistics of absent fathers in our society. Be that virtuous woman and the crown of your husband. Join the wagon of those who are happily married, and join in making marriages great again, especially in Christendom. Let nothing you've read in this book be taken as judgmental. If anything I've mentioned sounded as such, please forgive me. I wrote just as I was led, and you have every right to reject or condemn it. The overall aim is for you to help your husband start fulfilling his headship role. By so doing, he

> LET THIS BOOK SERVE AS A GUIDE AND AN INSIGHT THAT WILL HELP YOU UNDERSTAND YOUR HUSBAND AND HELP MOLD YOU INTO BECOMING A ROLE MODEL FOR OTHERS.

will help reduce the rising rate of fathers absent from homes in our communities. Men and their roles were addressed in my book *Not without the Head: An insightful guide for men to embrace God's instructions for success in marriage, family, and community.* I encourage you to read *Not without the Head* and you will surely understand my purpose in writing this book— *Understanding Your Husband.* Share this book if you were blessed, and let us hear your testimonies.

Shalom!

REVIEWS

Wow! This book is full of great insights and techniques to help us as ladies, wives, and women to relate well with our spouses. I love how my husband started this book by describing the two types of husbands we see homes, the outpouring man and the absorbing man. As a married woman, most likely you are married to one of these men and truthfully, it can be challenging at times. However, reading this book and putting into practice what's written will help you become that virtuous, supportive helper and a crown to your husband.

One thing that stands out for me as I read this book is in the area of submission. Yes! That big word—*submission*. My husband mentioned it takes one person to make a marriage work, not two, and I do agree with him. As a therapist, I now use this principle with my clients: for any marriage to succeed it will take one who is willing to keep the fire burning, and it does not matter whether is the woman or man. Yes, I know most times, as women, we think that if we have to give in all the time, it will give my husband an opportunity to use it as an advantage, but it's not so, especially if we see it from God's own perspective.

In Ephesians 5:22 it says, "Wives, submit yourselves to your own husbands as you do to the Lord (NIV)." That means I have a role to play in my marriage, which is to submit to my own husband. It took me a while to get this, because I felt submission was equal; after all, in verse 21 of Ephesians 5—it says submit to one another out of reverence for Christ. Therefore, if he is not submitting to me, why should I, and that's where we miss it as wives because we are now seeking and demanding our right.

God wants us as wives to submit to, honor, and respect our own husbands as we would do to the Lord. It is true that for wives, there are times we struggle to submit to our husbands because of past hurt, betrayal, and pain. The truth is that you cannot do it on your own; you need the Holy Spirit. He is the one that can help you to forgive and let go. The Holy Spirit will give you the grace to submit even though you, the wife, know that your husband does not deserve it. Today, I can graciously write that I don't struggle with submitting to or respecting my husband. I focus on those key words: "it takes one to make marriage work and submitting as you do to the Lord." And am enjoying my marriage; you too can enjoy this blessing if you're determined to put all you read in this book into practice.

Finally, I invite you to pray this prayer with me, believing that the Lord will do a new thing in your life, in the life of your husband, and in your marriage:

Lord Jesus, I need you in my heart. Come and take your place; heal my heart and make me whole once again. Help me, Lord, to forgive my husband (name) and let go of the past. Help me to begin to see him through the lens of your eyes. Help me to love my husband (name) from my heart, and give me your strength to honor, respect, and submit. Holy Spirit, fill me up with your love to overflowing, and when my husband (name) sees me, let him see your glory. Thank you, Lord, for bringing renewal, peace, and sweetness in my marriage and home in Jesus's name. Amen.

Ijeoma Ezeji-Okoye (wife of the author)
MA clinical psychology

***

Understanding one's husband is a journey and not a sprint. It is lifelong learning and discovery of the person that you have committed to doing life with through the ups and downs. In this book, Brother Fred, a seasoned marriage counselor and mentor to men, carefully examines foundational areas according to Scripture and God's design. He boldly addresses issues that many teachers may shy away from and confronts these areas with God's word.

This book is for every woman who aspires to be married or is already in a marriage and is seeking to understand and practice principles that produce a maximal relationship with her husband. Allow the Holy Spirit to take you on your own journey of discovery of what it truly means to be a helper to your husband in bringing out the very best in him. l encourage you to read it prayerfully, with an open mind. Use it as a guide, and let God show you areas of personal growth and development in your marriage. I pray that God's grace will cause you to flourish in your assignment to be the best cheerleader of your husband through the different seasons of life, in Jesus's Name!

Debo Ijiwola
Lead pastor, CityLight Church

***

Are you still struggling to understand your husband and why he does not seem to meet your expectations in your marriage, thereby causing pain, dissatisfaction, hatred, abandonment, separation, and divorce in some cases? I want you to relax, take a deep breath, and dive into this one-of-a-kind book written under the guidance of the Holy Spirit by a man who earnestly desires to see marriages succeed. If you were privileged to have read his book *Not Without the Head* you will agree with me that he has a way of communicating to both men and women with so much passion, honesty, and clarity that you will desire to know more. This book addresses spouses and singles, and you will do yourself a favor if you invest your time as well as act on the knowledge acquired.

Hosea 4:6 says, "My people are destroyed for lack of knowledge." "Knowledge is power." Through the help of the Holy Spirit, the author takes us on a journey to uncover the mystery man called husband.

Neither husbands nor wives chose their roles. They are God-given. It is God who confirmed that man needed help and gave him the wife to help him fulfill his roles. The key areas outlined in this book will help you to understand him, and by submitting to God's ordained order, you will fulfill God's purpose and become a role model for others. Let us embrace our unique role with gratitude, promote it, and celebrate these mystery men in our lives.

Mrs. Grace Bwanhot

***

Before reading *Understanding Your Husband* by Fredrick Ezeji-Okoye, I knew I was in for a challenge. I had previously read his very authentic, thought-provoking book titled *Not Without the Head*, which explores the core issues surrounding the absence of fathers in society. The exploration left me saying, "Yes, all men need to read this book." So, when the author presented his new book, *Understanding Your Husband*, I knew that I had to be prepared to challenge my views and thought process about my relationship with my husband and men in general. Reading *Understanding Your Husband*, I experienced a wonderful and fruitful blend of God's word and life experiences that challenged me to process more deeply the words love, submission, headship, and helper. The author's tone is curious, truth-seeking, and humble, which invited me to meditate more critically on my views of what it means to be a "helper" or "helpmate" and being submissive. You can say that as I was reading the book, I struggled with the *"my rights"* thinking patterns described in this book, which are defense mechanisms that both husbands and wives experience difficulty. I also found myself questioning the Holy Spirit as I sought to clarify thoughts that stirred anxiety in response to the realities presented. This book is a treasure to both single and married individuals. It engages the Word of God with real-life examples. Anyone seeking knowledge and understanding about relationships will find this book an excellent resource for practical learning that engages the foundational and transformational truths in God's Word. I agree with Mr. Ezeji-Okoye's vision to reduce the absentee father pandemic. I highly recommend this book as a premarriage and/or marriage counseling tool. I believe it is a tool that can serve as a preventative measure to eliminate future conflicts in relationships. It provides readers with great advice about relationships and equips them with the tools necessary to make adjustments in their love-walk.

Peace,
Udechukwu-Ezeka

***

In author Fredrick Ezeji-Okoye's compelling book *Understanding Your Husband*, wives are called on to understand and demonstrate the significant responsibility and role they have as a "helper." The author recognizes that fulfilling this role as helper is "no walk in the park" and would require another "Helper," the Holy Spirit to enable both wives and husbands to focus on fulfilling their responsibilities, rather than their rights, in order to ensure a peaceful home.

Reading the book *Understanding Your Husband*, confirmed a personal change in my new approach of being a "helper." The book challenged me to do my best as a "helper." If I am completely honest, although this book served as a confirmation, I also struggled while reading some of the chapters. It is not that *Understanding Your Husband* lacks truth. On the contrary, the author was careful to include relevant scriptures to support his ideas. I struggled with the tendency to focus on "my rights" (you will understand when you read the book), which enabled me to feel justified in my actions.

Who should read *Understanding Your Husband*? This book is for newlyweds, people in seasoned marriages, those who are engaged, and the single adult who desires to be married someday. This book will cause you to reflect and take personal inventory of yourself to be sure you are equipped with the mindset and heart posture necessary to understand your husband, be an influencer of virtue, and ultimately, reduce the alarming rates of absent fathers.

Adedoyin David

* * *

Understanding Your Husband

Reading *Not without the Head* did not disappoint, and *Understanding Your Husband* continues in that tradition of Brother Fred's honesty and transparency. I myself am the product of an absentee father and can relate to the effect it had on me as a child, but thanks be to God, that cycle has not continued into my adulthood.

My understanding of the significance of validating our husband's role of headship has increased. The examples in the book solidify the importance of building up and not tearing down our husbands; especially when you both do not see eye to eye. In the secular world, when there is conflict between coworkers, the boss intervenes. So, it is when conflict arises in marriages, we as wives seek out the "boss" of our spouses, who is God, with guidance from the Holy Spirit.

Brother Fred calls us wives out with this simple truth. In submitting to our husbands, we are in essence submitting ourselves to God. Women are leaders, but the headship role is ordained by God exclusively for our husbands. Brother Fred breaks down these principles not only with the word of God but also with his life as living testimony. His passion for encouraging strong marriages is paramount and unmeasurable in these trying times and in times yet to come. Wives (and husbands too), I challenge you to reflect on the scriptures in *Understanding Your*

Husband, and allow it to minister to what you know to be true deep down in your heart.

Ramonica David

* * *

Understanding Your Husband by Brother Fred Ezeji-Okoye is a highly refreshing, impactful, and much-needed book today, written specifically for wives who seek to have happy and thriving marriages from a godly perspective. In this book, Brother Fred unlocks the secrets of getting the best out of your man by understanding your husband's personality and walking in love and respect in your relationship, as well as providing practical tips to develop true partnership, oneness, love, and vulnerability in your relationship. Be ready to finish this book and become empowered to make a difference in your marriage.

Brother Fred has also shown through this book that wives have a vital role to play in helping their husbands to fulfill their God-given roles as heads of their homes, loving spouses, and present fathers. Women, be encouraged to take up this ministry of understanding your husbands better with intentionality and prayer, and by surrounding yourself with the wise counsel contained in this book. *Understanding Your Husband* also dispels common and popular myths women have wrongly believed that hold them back from experiencing God's best in their marriages.

Sometimes, as Brother Fred writes, it takes *one person* to make a change in a marriage. Decide to be that one person today by reading this book and sharing it with your network.

Osen Imoukhuede

* * *

Understanding Your Husband is a must-read for every Woman as it offers advice based on biblical principles that will help you maintain a happy home. You certainly will learn a thing or two that will benefit your marriage. I must say that you might find some of the recommended actions difficult or annoying and will ponder, "Why me?" I felt the same way but can testify to a particular piece of advice that worked for me, though it was hard to receive and follow initially. Remember, with God all things are possible. Knowledge is key! So, get reading sisters!

Noni Nnamani

***

I am honored to participate in reviewing this book, *Understanding Your Husband*. To the glory of God, I have been happily married for thirty-seven years and am blessed with six children, three grandchildren, and two unborn grandchildren due anytime soon.

The author, Evangelist Fred Ezeji-Okoye is a distinguished Christian preacher and speaker. He is also the author of the book *Not without the Head*, which is a guide for men to live by God's instructions in their marriages and homes.

The genesis of this book *Understanding Your Husband* arose when the author identified the need to encourage women to help their husbands fulfill their God-ordained role as the heads in their families. This book, which is primarily targeted at women, is aimed at showing them how they can enhance the harmony, togetherness, and joy of marriage.

I was thrilled with the book because it's educational and inspiring for spinsters and those young and old in marriage. Ladies, this book will help you journey through your marital issues, self-discovery, and perhaps healing/reconciliation. The book elucidates key points for a successful marriage, like good communication, listening, understanding, trust, respect, love, patience, and above all, prayers and fear of the

Lord. The book is nonjudgmental—it is written to bring out the best in marriage and advocates for successful marriages.

Ladies, you have the ability, and every step you take is a choice. Tell yourself you can do it, believing that with God everything is possible.

In my own journey, I learned that five love languages are powerful in marriage, and the author addresses all of them in this book. They are expression of affection, assisting in household chores, exchanging gifts, quality time together, and physical touch. It's advisable as an individual to learn your spouse's love language, because this will help you not to be emptying your tank in the wrong place.

In summary, the book guides you to be a woman who is very much "husband and family-oriented." Embrace your in-laws. Do your best and strive for peace. Create room for your husband to have full confidence in you, and I bet you'll overcome all trials and temptations. Nobody is perfect; try to work things out together. Perseverance is the key to your victory, irrespective of your challenges. The first five years of marriage are usually bumpy; so don't go to bed without resolving any problems. Put Jesus Christ first just like Mary, the sister of Martha, and emulate some amazing women of God in the Bible like Deborah, who was a compassionate leader, Esther, who was brave, etc. Pray together and ask for forgiveness. There's a saying, "The family that prays together stays together." Make your home a holy family. Ladies, you're more precious than rubies (Prov. 3:15).

The book advises you to not neglect your appearance; to be at your Sunday best every day. Love yourself so you can give love to your family. When you look at the challenges, tell yourself, "I can do all things through Christ who strengthens me (Phil. 4:13)."

The book is loaded with quotes from Bible verses relevant to each chapter and content. I urge you to also remember these Bible verses:

– Prov.11:16 "Honor goes to the kind and gracious woman."

– Prov.19:14 "Houses and riches are the inheritance of fathers but a prudent wife is from the Lord."

– Psalm 46:5 "God is in the midst of her, she shall not be moved, God will help her when morning dawns."

Lady Lynda

***

This book is truly one of the best I have read that truly explains the subject of submission in marriage in light of the New Testament.

Great insight reveals that the man and the woman are equal but have different roles. The man is not elected to be a leader by man, but from the beginning, God made it so.

To be submissive to a husband does not make the woman inferior to the man in any way. Rather, it means that the woman acknowledges the leadership or headship of her husband and honors God's order of creation.

When the woman understands that she is modeling the role of the church submitting to Jesus, she will, by all means, embrace submission with joy. When a wife and mother accepts her role to submit to her husband, she will not only create peace and harmony in the home but will keep the man home as a father for the children. No more absentee fathers!

Understanding that submission is key in sustaining any marriage will reduce the rate of divorce. Of course, there is the place of submitting one to another (Ephesians 5:21), but knowing or acknowledging where to draw the line is very important. As a wife and a *believer*, understanding that what Jesus has done for me, the extent of His love, will open my heart to accept my role as a submissive wife. We can only receive what Christ has done in the posture of submission. So also, to have the benefits of marriage, one must submit to the head.

I cannot agree more with the author: "If wives respect their husbands, the man will function well in his headship role."

Thank you, Brother Fred Ezeji-Okoye, for breaking down in simple terms the meaning and benefits of submission of the woman in marriage. Two become one, equal, but with different roles or functions, for the proper running of the home.

Praying that there will be fewer and fewer absentee fathers, in Jesus's Name.

Great book, great insight. Truly a blessing.

Pastor Rhoda Dibie

***

Reading through *Understanding Your Husband* brings to the fore how fighting for our "rights" while ignoring our responsibilities as wives (or husbands) is wrong. The author articulates how our lives as wives should be regulated by the Word of God, not by the acts of men, i.e., our husbands. It was a good reminder that men did not lobby for the headship role—rather it was God-ordained. I recommend this book to wives who truly want to be united to—not untied from—their husbands. Together, you will achieve more than either of you could achieve separately. You are better together.

Ada Adeleke-Kelani (aka Quip Queen)
author of *101 Quips and Quotes That Will Strengthen and Sweeten Your Marriage and Family Relationships*

NOTES

NOTES

NOTES

NOTES

ABOUT THE AUTHOR

Fredrick K. Ezeji-Okoye is the author of *Who Prays for the Pastor*. He is a communicator at heart with a passion to share the Gospel both orally and in writing. Among his many gifts and talents, he is a minister, writer, and motivational speaker with a mandate to equip and empower the body of Christ by igniting a greater thirst and hunger for God's word and intercessory prayer.

He is the founder and president of "The Men of Faith Network," a fast-growing, diverse, and multicultural network of pastors and leaders with global outreach. Fredrick is the CEO of The Liberty Foundation LLC, a company that specializes in training church workers and consultants. He lives in the Chicago metro area with his wife Ijeoma and their three children, Chisom, Nkiruka, and Chinenye.

www.menoffaithnetwork.org
https://libertyfoundationllc.com/

Be sure to read the companion title book by Bro. Fredrick Ezeji-Okoye

Discover your inner strengths; learn the value and importance of being present for your family as the head. Embrace the plan God intended for you—as the head of your family, providing the leadership needed for a strong and godly marriage and family, for home is the foundation for the larger community in the world. **Not without the Head is a timely guide that invites you to take up this role and to embrace how important you are to the building of this foundation, as it cannot succeed without the head!**

With this insightful book, author Brother Frederick Ezeji-Okoye brings God's instruction to life, offering personal experiences as examples of how to successfully apply these steps, while navigating through day-to-day encounters. The author shares his vision of this life so men can take up their role as the head—as man submits to Christ's leadership as head of all. Armed with these practical tools and personal perspectives, the reader can envision this role as a reality in his own life—leading as head, living God's plan for man.

CPSIA information can be obtained
at www.ICGtesting.com
Printed in the USA
JSHW032040260222
23341JS00006B/8

9 781952 025747